D1520888

Haunted Presence

The Numinous in Gothic Fiction

S. L. Varnado

THE UNIVERSITY OF ALABAMA PRESS
Tuscaloosa and London

PR
830
. S85
V37
1987

Library of Congress Cataloging-in-Publication Data

Varnado, S. L., 1929–
  Haunted presence.

  Bibliography: p.
  Includes index.
  1. English fiction—History and criticism.
2. Supernatural in literature. 3. American fiction—
History and criticism. 4. Gothic revival (Literature)
5. Ghost stories, English—History and criticism.
6. Ghost stories, American—History and criticism.
I. Title.
PR830.S85V37   1987   823'.0872'09   86-16050
ISBN 0-8173-0324-3

British Library Cataloguing-in-Publication Data is available.

To my wife, Mary Lou

Contents

Acknowledgments   ix
1 The Literature of the Supernatural   1
2 The Numinous   8
3 The Gothic Novel   20
4 Frankenstein   42
5 Poe and Initiation into the Sacred   60
6 The Numinous Aesthetic of Henry James   77
7 The Daemonic in *Dracula*   95
8 The Modern Period   115
9 Analyzing the *mysterium tremendum*   130
   Notes   134
   Bibliography   149
   Index   156

Acknowledgments

I would like to thank the administration of the University of South Alabama for the grant that made possible the writing of this book. I also wish to thank Professor G. R. Thompson, who encouraged me; Debra E. Hopkins, who typed the manuscript; and my wife, who proofread it.

Haunted Presence

1

The Literature of the Supernatural

In this book I attempt to analyze and interpret the literature of the supernatural by means of certain insights derived from what today is generally referred to as the "philosophy of religious experience." Such an approach is not unknown in present-day literary studies.[1] My task here is unique, however, in that I make use of the ideas of a particular theologian, Rudolf Otto, whose profound description of the numinous, set forth in his *Idea of the Holy,* illuminates what I take to be the very essence of the supernatural tale.[2] I shall argue that Otto's account of the *mysterium tremendum et fascinans,* with its associated categories of the sacred and the profane, defines the purpose and the aesthetic value of such literature.

Although Otto's work has received wide recognition in modern scholarly circles, the term he coined to express the supernatural element in experience—the numinous—has passed into general use in a highly amorphous form. Nowadays, it is used to describe anything from a ghost to a movie idol to a computer. In my view, this situation is unfortunate.

Otto's analysis of religious experience is quite specific and, in my estimation, profound; it deserves better than it has received. In fact, one of my subsidiary purposes in this book is to correct misinterpretations of Otto's work and thus rescue it from the vagaries of media language. My primary interest, however, lies in the literature of the supernatural. My study encompasses the Gothic novel of the eighteenth century in addition to representative ghostly tales of the nineteenth and twentieth centuries.

Until recent times, the supernatural tale has received little serious attention from literary critics. G. R. Thompson gives what must certainly be the correct explanation of this neglect: "Until the 1950's, the prevailing critical view of Gothic literature was essentially that of the later nineteenth-century moralists: namely that the Gothic lacked 'high seriousness.' "[3] Despite its antiquity, wide geographical distribution, and continuing popularity, the ghostly tale has often been looked upon as a literary curiosity, half-art, half-anthropology.

Such a critical attitude is not difficult to understand. The ghost story, by its very nature, maintains only the weakest connections with the central themes of mainstream literature: romantic love, conflict between man and man, greed, ambition, political questions, and the like. It is true that in a few ghost stories, the protagonist falls in love with a ghost. When that has happened, the romance generally has been doomed to failure. In such cases, courtship is difficult and marriage is out of the question. In the supernatural tale, conflict takes on a peculiar form as well. The conflict usually is a matter of pursuit, on the one hand, and retreat, on the other. One "runs" from a ghost; if there is to be any sort of confrontation, it must be carried out with amulets, spells, incantations—objects not within the inventory of most people.

Supernatural literature is often said to lack high seriousness or moral purpose. In the most common ghost stories, the human protagonist is often an innocent victim who blunders into the occult dimension. The protagonist is a harmless, conventional individual who may be on holiday, sitting quietly in an easy chair, inspecting an old house, or walking through a forest. He or she has done nothing "wrong" in the usual sense; quite often the ghost that the protagonist encounters teaches no moral lesson or lessons. Moral neutrality in these tales sometimes extends to the supernatural creatures of the tales. If the ghosts are seldom exactly benign, they are frequently less than evil; and when they *are* evil, their evil is not of the ordinary variety. Ghosts rarely steal anything of value, seldom use bad language, kill less often than one might suppose, and are almost universally chaste. If they sometimes emit an aura of pure evil, the evil is not the sort that would bring them to the attention of the police. For the most part, spirits pursue interests of their own, devoid of moral calculation, such as retrieving a key, a ring, or a lock of hair. When, on occasion, they kill, it is often simply by frightening their victim to death; their greatest mischief is that most conventional of misdemeanors— disturbing the peace.

If, in the past, the ghost story has occupied a peripheral position in literature, however, it has never suffered from neglect by the public. From earliest history, the ghostly tale has enjoyed popularity; nor is it difficult to imagine our Neanderthal ancestors slinking timorously to their caves after the shaman had delivered a particularly frightening tale around the campfire. Supernatural elements, in fact, abound in classical literature, as seen in the *Odyssey,* the *Aeneid, Beowulf,* the poems of Chaucer, and *Sir Gawain and the Green Knight;* they are staples in the dramas of Marlowe, Kyd, and Shakespeare and in the poetry of Spenser. In the eighteenth century the supernatural tale took on a distinct form, becoming the Gothic novel; in the nineteenth century we meet it in the work of Sir Walter Scott, Samuel Taylor Coleridge, Charles Dickens, Edgar Allan Poe, Wilkie Collins, Joseph Le Fanu, Oscar Wilde, and others. In our own time, the supernatural story has prospered not only in literature but also in motion pictures and television, to the point of sometimes being trivialized.

One anomaly of ghostly literature is that, while most people will admit to an enjoyment of the genre, the admission is often tinged with embarrassment. "I don't believe in ghosts, but I like ghost stories," is a formula on the lips of people whose views range from the mystical to the materialistic. Nor can one doubt that literary ghosts linger in thoroughly unregimented form in communist countries.

In other words, the genre of occult literature contains paradoxes. On the one hand, it is sometimes considered a fugitive form which is less than respectable; on the other, its popularity remains undimmed. One might be inclined to write off the paradox as an example of mankind's love of fantasy; but that would mean lumping the ghost story together with the fairy tale, the myth, and the legend. The problem with such a view is that the ghost story does not fit comfortably in the general classification of fantasy; it is somehow "different." One feels the difference. It is as though the ghost story occupied an ontological plane different from other kinds of fantasy.

Because the argument I pursue in this book to some degree hinges on this difference, the matter requires exploration. We can begin by stating that fantasy is a form of literature requiring an act of the imagination rather than one of the intellect. In such fantasies as Tolkien's *The Hobbit* and C. S. Lewis's *Narnia* stories, such myths as *The Golden Fleece,* and the fairy tale "The Sleeping Beauty," the reader is asked for imaginative sympathy rather than intellectual assent. The mental reaction is: "How delightful if such things could happen, but I know they can't."

For this reason, fantasy makes few demands in regard to realism. The elements in a fantasy (flying carpets, dragons, unicorns, elves, fairy godmothers) are created from objects the reader has knowledge of or experience of in real life, but now they are joined into new forms under pressure from the imagination. A dragon, for example, is simply a large, reptilian creature that has wings and breathes fire, elements that, if never joined together in reality, are nevertheless readily synthesized by the imagination. The writer of a fantasy is free to make a dragon realistic (as Spenser does in *The Faerie Queene*); or the writer may, as is done in most fantasies, simply postulate a dragon and let it go at that. In either case, no act of intellectual assent is required of the reader. Rather, he or she is invited to enter a world of heightened experience, a world consisting of familiar objects that have been transformed into new shapes and to some degree "stretched." The question of the reality of these fantastic creatures does not arise. If it does, the story ceases to be a fantasy.

Such is not the case with supernatural tales, however. In these stories we have a distinct element of feeling which is not drawn from ordinary, or "natural," experience but which nevertheless evokes an echo from the reader's sense of reality. The reader of a ghost story may never have seen a ghost, may, in fact, be a thoroughgoing materialist. Unless this reader can summon up a feeling that something "ghostly" *might* exist, however, the story will carry no interest or meaning. Like Hippolyta in *A Midsummer Night's Dream,* the reader will say: "This is the silliest stuff that ever I heard."

That is why *realism* is the sine qua non of the ghostly tale and why writers of such tales work hard to create the proper sense of verisimilitude. The ghost story stands or falls on its power to convince the reader that the *feeling of the supernatural* corresponds to some element in reality. This, in fact, may be close to what Coleridge meant when he spoke of "that willing suspension of disbelief." The suspension of disbelief is a thoroughly different act from that required by mere fantasy.

The ghost story, in short, presents the reader with what can best be described as an ontological challenge. The challenge is not in the form of philosophical propositions, however; it is in the form of feelings and emotions, but feelings and emotions that maintain a connection with the sense of reality.

It is at this point that the insights of Rudolf Otto prove most useful. I shall argue that the area of reality that Otto called the numinous—the *feeling* of the supernatural—stands at the center of Gothic literature. An understanding of this unique category of experience, along with its associated concept of "the sacred and the profane," will, I hope, clarify the purpose of ghostly literature and demonstrate the high seriousness referred to above.

The use of Otto's theory in the study of supernatural literature is a relatively new and untapped field. Except for a brief, albeit seminal, discussion by Devendra Varma, an essay of mine, and a few scattered references in Barton St. Armand's study of the fiction of H. P. Lovecraft, the question has scarcely been treated.[4] Consequently, my purpose here is to break new ground; I have therefore rigorously limited myself to "representative" works of Gothic fiction.

In writing this book I have not attempted a history of Gothic literature. Many such histories exist, and anyone in search of more extensive, detailed accounts of the genre will have no difficulty finding them.[5] In presenting my case for numinous literature, I have omitted several major writers whose work, in part at least, might well have been discussed. Certain works by Sir Walter Scott, Charles Dickens, Nathaniel Hawthorne, Herman Melville, Robert Louis Stevenson, Oscar Wilde, and Joseph Conrad contain distinct numinous elements; in my judgment, however, this interest is never central. Other writers, omitted with regret, are Joseph Sheridan Le Fanu, Edward George Bulwer-Lytton, Charles Brockden Brown, Ambrose Bierce, and M. R. James. The work of these men is clearly numinous and, in some cases, of high merit; but in my estimation, none of them added any distinct or original development to the Gothic tradition, being content to work with themes and techniques already established.

The writers whose works I have selected for analysis were chosen according to three precisely defined principles: first, they exhibit as their main interest the sense of the numinous; second, each introduced new themes or techniques which were to become representative; third, all have attained a secure place within the genre of the occult.

The study begins with writers of the classical Gothic period: Horace Walpole, Ann Radcliffe, M. G. Lewis, and Charles Maturin. Later chapters deal with Mary Shelley, Edgar Allan Poe, Henry James, and Bram Stoker. The final chapter takes up three modern Gothic writers: Arthur Machen, Algernon Blackwood, and H. P. Lovecraft.

Before beginning my analysis of these authors, I wish to devote the following chapter to a discussion of Rudolf Otto's concept of the numinous as set forth in *The Idea of the Holy* and other works.

2

The Numinous

Everyone who has given the matter some consideration is aware of a great and overriding division in our mental lives. The two parts of this division have received a variety of names through the years without losing their identity. Generally speaking, these parts may be called *reason* and *intuition;* but a large and confusing array of synonyms has attached itself to each part. Modern psychology since Freud refers to them as the "conscious" and the "unconscious" parts of the mind. In the nineteenth century the terms *understanding* and *imagination* were preferred. The medieval Scholastics knew these distinctions; there is an echo of them in Anselm's formula *fides quarens intellectum.* Some other terms for reason would be *thought, knowledge, logic,* and *science;* for intuition we might substitute *faith, mysticism, instinct, heart,* and *feeling.*

Although the terminology surrounding these two forms of cognition is at times obscure, the reality underlying them is not. The term *reason* obviously refers to that portion of our mental life about which we can form clear concepts and

8

explicit judgments. The term *intuition,* on the other hand, suggests an immediate cognitive knowledge, the grounds of which cannot be made conceptual. Emerson called the latter "instinct" and "spontaneity." It is Newman's "illative sense," Augustine's "illumination"; and it resonates in Pascal's epigram, "The heart has its reasons which the reason knows nothing of."

It is with this second category of mental experience—intuition—that the work of Rudolf Otto (1860–1937) is concerned. In his years as a professor of theology at Marburg University, Otto's studies of Luther, Kant, and Schleiermacher turned his interest toward what we would today term the "psychology of religious experience." The subject has been illuminated since Otto's time by the work of Henri Bergson, Mircea Eliade, and others; but when Otto began his studies it was virtual terra incognita.

Otto set out to explore the essence of the religious impulse as it appeared in mankind's emotional life and feelings. Since the area he was concerned with is to some extent independent of concepts, Otto called it "the non-rational." In his classic *The Idea of the Holy* he says: "This book, recognizing the profound import of the non-rational for metaphysic, makes a serious attempt to analyze all the more exactly the feeling which remains where the concept fails."[1]

Searching for a term by which to characterize the nonrational aspect of religion, Otto began with the category of the holy *(das heilige).* Holiness, he observes, is a category of interpretation "peculiar to the sphere of religion." The holy includes ethical and rational concepts but also contains a specific element, or "moment," which sets it aside from the purely intellectual. This ineffable, or nonrational, element in the holy "eludes apprehension in terms of concepts."[2]

In order to describe this ineffable element in the holy—this "unnamed Something"—Otto was forced to invent a new term, to find a word to stand for this element in isolation, this "extra" in the meaning of "holy" above and beyond the meaning of goodness. For this purpose I adopt a word coined from the Latin *numen. Omen* has given us "ominous," and there is no reason why from *numen* we should not similarly form a word "numinous." I shall speak, then, of a unique "numinous" category of value and of a definitely "numinous" state of mind, which is always found wherever the category is applied. This mental state is perfectly *sui generis* and irreducible to any other; and therefore, like every absolutely primary and elementary datum, while it admits of being discussed, it cannot be strictly defined.

Because the numinous cannot be fully described by concepts, Otto suggests that the reader "direct his mind to a moment of deeply felt religious experience, as little as possible qualified by other forms of consciousness." The feeling-state that results consists of a number of distinct yet harmonious elements (or "moments," as Otto prefers) which can be expressed by means of an ideogram—a symbolic phrase that, by analogy, suggests the numinous experience. For this purpose he chooses the Latin phrase *mysterium tremendum et fascinans,* "a frightening yet fascinating mystery."

In attempting to analyze the numinous emotion by means of this ideogram, Otto starts with the qualifying adjective "tremendum." *Tremor* is the Latin word for "fear," but Otto uses this merely "natural" fear to suggest "a quite specific kind of emotional response, wholly distinct from that of being afraid." It is, in fact, more akin to dread or awe, and such words as the German *Scheu* (dread) and *grasslich* (grisly) or the English *uncanny* come closest to expressing its meaning. Physical reactions to this moment of numinous consciousness are as "unnatural" as the emotion itself. Otto mentions such phrases as "my blood ran icy cold," and "my flesh crept," adding, "anyone who is capable of more precise introspection must recognize that the distinction between such a 'dread' and natural fear is not simply one of degree and intensity. The awe or 'dread' *may* indeed be so overwhelmingly great that it seems to penetrate to the very marrow, making the man's hair bristle and his limbs quake. But it may also steal upon him almost unobserved. . . ." In contrast, merely natural fear may contain nothing of the numinous emotion. "I may be beyond all measure afraid and terrified without there being even a trace of the feeling of uncanniness in my emotion."

The distinction between "natural" emotion and numinous emotion is crucial to understanding Otto's theory. A passage from C. S. Lewis's *The Problem of Pain* offers a clear explanation of the distinction:

> Those who have not met this term [the *numinous*] may be introduced to it by the following device. Suppose you were told that there was a tiger in the next room: you would know that you were in danger and would probably feel fear. But if you were told "There is a ghost in the next room," and believed it, you would feel, indeed, what is often called fear, but of a different kind. It would not be based on the knowledge of danger, for no one is primarily afraid of what a ghost may do to him, but of the mere fact that it is a ghost. It is "uncanny" rather than dangerous, and the special kind of fear it excites may be called Dread. With the Uncanny one has reached the fringes of the Numinous. Now suppose that you were told simply "There is a mighty spirit in the room" and believed it. Your feelings would then be even less like the mere fear of danger: but the disturbance would be profound. You would feel wonder and a certain shrinking—a sense of inadequacy to cope with such a visitant and of prostration before it. . . . This feeling may be described as awe, and the object which excites it is the Numinous.[3]

In addition to the note of awe emphasized by Lewis, Otto distinguishes two other unique feeling-states suggested by the Latin word *tremendum.* The first he calls *majestas:* a sense of might, power, or "absolute overpoweringness." The subject perceiving this numinous emotion experiences a sense of "creature consciousness," of being "dust and ashes," and of sheer self-depreciation. The feeling is especially strong in certain forms of mysticism and by analogy is related to the sense of religious humility.[4]

A third element called forth by the *tremendum* is the "energy" or "urgency" of the numinous. The feeling is associated symbolically with expressions of God's vitality, passion, emotional temper, will, force, impetus. This feeling finds expression in the biblical concept of the "wrath" of God. Otto associates it as well with Fichte's *Absolute* and with Schopenhauer's *Will.* Goethe calls it the "daemonic." It is, Otto contended, at the root of all "voluntaristic" mysticism in which God is perceived as a "consuming fire." The sense of urgency—the daemonic—is strong among primitive religions but does not die out in more advanced ones.

These three affective states—awe, majesty, and overpoweringness—are suggested by the adjective *tremendum* which, in turn, qualifies the substantive *mysterium.* Otto describes the *mysterium* as the form of the numinous experience. "Conceptually," he says, *"mysterium* denotes merely that which is hidden and esoteric, that which is beyond conception or understanding, extraordinary and unfamiliar. The term does not define the object more positively in its qualitative character. But though what is enunciated in the word is negative, what is meant is something absolutely and intensely positive. This pure positive we can experience in feelings."

The feeling evoked by the *mysterium* can best be described by the word *stupor.* "It signifies blank wonder, astonishment that strikes us dumb, amazement absolute." The feeling is associated with the theological term *the wholly other (alienum),* "that which is quite beyond the sphere of the usual, the intelligible, and the familiar." It is associated on the purely natural plane with objects that are puzzling, astounding, or surprising. As is the case with purely natural fear, however, the emotion quickly passes over into something qualitatively different from mere natural bewilderment.

To clarify his meaning Otto analyzes the "fear of ghosts." The real attraction of a ghost, he says, "consists in this, that of itself and in an uncommon degree it entices the imagination, awakening strong interest and curiosity: it is the weird thing itself that allures the fancy. . . . [It] is a thing which 'doesn't really exist at all', the 'wholly other', something which has no place in our scheme of reality."

These several "moments" *(mysterium tremendum)* now combine with a third moment, one which Otto designates by the word *fascinans*. *Fascinans* is at the opposite pole from the daunting aspect of *numinous*. It is the attracting or fascinating side of the numinous, "a bliss which embraces all those blessings that are indicated or suggested in positive fashion by any 'doctrine of salvation,' and it quickens all of them through and through; but these do not exhaust it. Rather, by its all pervading, penetrating glow it makes of these very blessings more than the intellect can conceive in them or affirm of them." The combination of feelings evoked by these seemingly opposite states of numinous consciousness results in a strange "harmony of contrasts":

> These two qualities, the daunting and the fascinating, now combine in a strange harmony of contrasts, and the resultant dual character of the numinous consciousness . . . is at once the strangest and most noteworthy phenomenon in the whole history of religion. The daemonic-divine object may appear to the mind an object of horror and dread, but at the same time it is no less something that allures with a potent charm, and the creature, who trembles before it, utterly cowed and cast down, has always at the same time the impulse to turn

to it, nay even to make it somehow his own. The "mystery" is for him not merely something to be wondered at but something that entrances him; and beside that in it which bewilders and confounds, he feels a something that captivates and transports him with a strange ravishment, rising often enough to the pitch of dizzy intoxication; it is the Dionysiac-element in the numen.

This, in essence, is Otto's conception of the numinous. To grasp it fully, however, it is necessary to understand what he means in calling it an a priori concept. "The facts of the numinous consciousness point therefore . . . to a hidden substantive source, from which the religious ideas and feelings are formed, which lies in the mind independently of sense experience." This does not mean, however, that the numinous is a mere subjective feeling. Quite the opposite is true. The very nature of the numinous experience is such that it cannot be perceived unless the subject feels that there is indeed something objective before which he is a creature. To clarify the point, Otto cites William James's *The Varieties of Religious Experience:*

> It is as if there were in the human consciousness a sense of reality, a feeling of objective presence, a perception of what we may call "something there" more deep and more general than any of the special and particular "senses" by which the current psychology supposes existent realities to be originally revealed.[5]

The importance of this sense of objectivity in the numinous cannot be overstressed, especially in considering its literary and artistic applications. The writer of numinous literature can produce the proper effects only if he or she convinces the reader, at least transiently, that the numinous reality exists independently of the self. In this sense, the writer's task is more demanding than that of the writer of fantasy, who is in no way constrained to make the reader believe in the imaginative object, whether a giant, dragon, or magic carpet.

The numinous, then, can be summed up as an affective state in which the percipient—through feelings of awe, mystery, and fascination—becomes aware of an objective spiritual presence. Otto would argue that the feeling is universal, that it exists in both primitive and more highly developed religions.

Throughout *The Idea of the Holy,* Otto emphasizes his contention that the numinous is not identical with the fully developed category of the holy. The concept of holiness must of necessity include theological and moral elements. The numinous may, in fact, exist in a form detached from the category of The Holy. As we will see below, it may even take on the aspect of what Otto calls "the negative numinous," in which the daemonic element is emphasized. Thus it seems clear that the experience may further the analysis of literary and artistic works not generally conceived of as religious. For what else is one to say of the castles and mountain crags of Mrs. Radcliffe's novels, the glaciers, ice floes, and desolate Scottish islands of *Frankenstein* or the spectral seascapes of *The Narrative of Authur Gordon Pym* but that they summon up the precise moods and feelings Otto described? By using Otto's insights we can sense a new, more profound note in certain literary works which in the past have been viewed with bewilderment or even condescension by certain critics.

Another fruitful link between supernatural literature and the numinous appears in Otto's discussion of preternatural events and magic. The preternatural in Gothic literature has been a source of dismay to many critics. It does, indeed, require a strong palate to absorb all the bleeding portraits, animate skeletons, lycanthropes, rattling chains, and vampires that infest the older Gothic novels; but artistic use of the preternatural should not, in itself, form a barrier to critical appreciation of Gothicism. It is on this point that Otto supplies a useful apologetic: "Now the magical is nothing but a suppressed and dimmed form of the numinous, a crude form of it which great art purifies and ennobles." He adds,

> To us of the West the Gothic appears as the most numinous of all types of art. This is due in the first place to its sublimity; but Worringer in his *Problem der Ghotik* has done a real service in showing that the peculiar impressiveness of Gothic does not consist in its sublimity alone, but draws upon a strain inherited from primitive magic, of which he tries to show the historical derivation.[6]

The magical or preternatural, if used artistically, may serve to reinforce the numinous effect of a work. For this reason, the exploration of the magical in certain ghostly tales forms one of the major tasks of this work.

The Idea of the Holy contains chapters of special interest to the literary critic on the artistic means of arousing the numinous consciousness. "Of directer methods our Western art has only two," Otto remarks, "and they are in a noteworthy way negative, viz., *darkness* and *silence.*" Otto's discussion of the artistic use of darkness conjures up numerous images of the "haunted castle" theme so familiar in the Gothic novel: "The semi-darkness that glimmers in vaulted halls, or beneath the branches of a lofty forest glade, strangely quickened and stirred by the mysterious play of half-lights, has always spoken eloquently to the soul, and the builders of temples, mosques and churches have made full use of it." Silence is "what corresponds to this in the language of musical sounds. . . . It is a spontaneous reaction to the feeling of the actual *numen praesens.*" Both artistic means are native to Western art; but Oriental art, Otto says, makes continual use of a third, namely, empty distance and emptiness.

Empty distance, remote vacancy, is, as it were, the sublime in the horizontal. The wide-stretching desert, the boundless uniformity of the steppe, have a real sublimity, and even in us Westerners they set vibrating chords of the numinous along with the note of the sublime, according to the principle of association of feelings.

From the preceding discussion it is arguable that Otto's concept of the numinous provides insights into the spirit of Gothic and supernatural literature. Mountain gloom, lonely castles, phantom ships, violent storms, and the vastness of sea and polar regions correspond closely to Otto's depiction of numinous reality. Similarly, the preternatural machinery of Gothic fiction and ghostly tales—whether magical lore, apparitions, ghouls, vampires, or revenants—finds its justification not in an overripe fantasy, but in an effort to evoke that profound effect which Otto termed *mysterium tremendum*.

In addition to its function as an ontological reality, the concept of the numinous takes into account another puzzling aspect of supernatural literature, namely, its supposed moral ambivalence or neutrality. As I have explained, the ghostly tale often appears to be devoid of ethical content. In such tales the encounter between a human protagonist and a supernatural agent often has the appearance of being due to the merest chance and seems to result in no significant ethical conclusion. At a very superficial level, one might be tempted to write the ghost story off with the formula: "Boy meets ghost, boy flees ghost, boy escapes ghost."

It is in answer to such problems that Otto's ideas may prove useful, for Otto held that the numinous is not confined to ontological reality but also has an axiological, or value-oriented, character. That is to say, the numinous contains a value category in its own right and as a consequence may be used to analyze certain moral problems, albeit of a rather fugitive nature.

According to Otto, the numinous experience in itself has no ethical character in the conventional sense and may exist independently of all moral systems. This is evident in certain primitive religions where the numinous object appears to be "beyond good and evil." It is only in a later development, when the numinous is commingled with moral and rational elements, that it becomes part of the fully developed category of The Holy.

On the other hand, even in its pure form and without moral connotations, the numinous remains permeated by certain obscure "value elements." This is seen most clearly in what Otto calls the sense of "creature feeling" that the numinous object evokes in the subject perceiving it. Confronted by the numinous object (the sacred), the subject feels himself or herself "profane."

> This sanctus is not merely "perfect" or "beautiful" or "sublime" or "good," though being like these concepts also a value, objective and ultimate, it has a definite, perceptible analogy with them. It is the positive numinous value or worth, and to it corresponds on the side of the creature a numinous disvalue or "unworth."

The sense of numinous value, the sacred, is recognized as standing outside the sphere of morality as such.

> In every highly developed religion the appreciation of moral obligation and duty ranking as a claim of the deity upon man has been developed side by side with the religious feeling itself. Nonetheless, a profoundly humble and heart-felt recognition of "the holy" may occur in particular experiences without being always definitely charged or infused with the sense of moral demands.

Nor is the opposite pole, the sense of numinous "disvalue" or the *profane,* intrinsically a moral category. "Mere 'unlawfulness' only becomes 'sin,' 'impiety,' 'sacrilege,' when the character of *numinous unworthiness* or *disvalue* goes on to be transferred to and centered in moral delinquency."

Admittedly, the theory of numinous value and disvalue is debatable; but as a description of phenomenological realities, it is convincing. As such, it applies very well to certain Gothic and supernatural tales which will be under discussion. Employing Otto's categories of numinous value and disvalue, I hope to throw light on the supposed moral neutrality of certain supernatural themes as they appear in the writings of Poe, in Mary Shelley's *Frankenstein,* and in Henry James's *The Turn of the Screw.*

Since Otto's death in 1937, his ideas, as set forth in *The Idea of the Holy* and later works, have been appropriated by a number of theologians, anthropologists, psychologists, and historians of religion.[7] In addition, literary critics have pointed out numinous elements in Shakespeare, the Romantics, and other writers.[8]

It is upon such a system of thought—profound and original—that this survey of Gothic literature is conducted.

3

The Gothic Novel

A degree of paradox is evident in the fact that the first sustained example of what I have chosen to call numinous literature, Horace Walpole's *Castle of Otranto* (1764), was created during that most rationalistic of historical periods—the Enlightenment. At the very time when neo-classicism, liberalism, and scientific inquiry were becoming established among the intellectuals of Europe, Walpole's dark vision of the nonrational appeared, demanding attention and instigating a new movement.

In his *The Sacred and the Profane,* the noted historian of religion Mircea Eliade suggests a possible motive for this sudden awakening.[1] Modern societies of the West, Eliade says, have seen the development of what he calls "nonreligious man." In these societies nonreligious man regards himself as the sole agent in history, refusing to admit the influence of transcendent forces. Such a man, however, is the descendant of earlier religious traditions of his ancestors and cannot entirely free himself from them. He is the product of his past, and emotional traces of that past remain in him.

"To acquire a world of his own," Eliade says, "he has desacralized the world in which his ancestors lived; but to do so he has been obliged to adopt the opposite of an earlier type of behavior, and that behavior is still emotionally present to him, in one form or another, ready to be reactualized in his deepest being."[2]

Significantly, Walpole's work began as a dream. "I waked one morning," he wrote later in a note to *The Castle of Otranto,*

> from a dream of which all I could recover was that I had thought myself in an ancient castle (a very natural dream for a head filled like mine with Gothic story) and that on the uppermost bannister of the great staircase I saw a gigantic hand in armour. In the evening I sat down, and began to write, without knowing in the least what I intended to say or relate.[3]

The novel that resulted established a new literary movement that was to last for almost a century. It also created a basic pattern for what I shall call "numinous literature." This was no small accomplishment, and if later generations find *The Castle of Otranto* a bit absurd in places,[4] we must constantly remind ourselves of the sheer originality of its conception.

The originality lay in Walpole's strategy of bringing together two distinct kinds of romance, the ancient and the modern. The ancient tradition, he says in the preface, was "all imagination and improbability," whereas the latter was realistic and credible but lacked imagination, adhering too closely to "common life."[5] Although he specifies no particular work, we can hazard a guess that by "ancient romance" Walpole is thinking of the Arthurian cycle, and by "modern romance" he refers to the novels of Fielding and Richardson.

Sir Walter Scott, who appropriated certain Gothic elements in his own novels, was an admirer of *The Castle of Otranto* and recommended Walpole's method of producing works in this genre. According to Scott, Walpole's aim was to appeal to "that secret and reserved feeling of love for the marvellous and supernatural which occupies a hidden corner in almost everyone's bosom."[6] It was the "art of exciting surprise and horror." Scott, however, clearly was aware of the epistemological problem in works of this kind. "The natural parts of the narrative are so contrived," he said, "that they associate themselves with the marvellous occurrences; and, by the force of that association, render those *speciosa miracula* striking and impressive, though our cooler reason admits their impossibility."[7] By fidelity to natural events and realism of description, the reader is prepared "gradually for the favorable reception of prodigies which, though they could not really have happened at any period, were consistent with the belief of all mankind at that in which the action is placed."[8]

Scott may have had a vague notion of the ontological realities that lie behind the preternaturalism of Walpole's novel. "By his too frequent recurrence of his prodigies, Mr. Walpole ran, perhaps, his greatest risk of awakening *la raison froide,* that cold common sense which he justly deemed the greatest enemy of the effect which he hoped to produce."[9] In other words, the superabundance of occult events can remove from the work the possibility of any sort of ontological reality, leaving only a residue of fantasy.

Ironically, it is the "prodigies" in the book that captured the imagination of eighteenth-century readers and that still impress modern critics. Devendra Varma compared these preternatural elements to the techniques of modern surrealists.[10] And Judith Wilt says of *Otranto:* "Its merits are not in character, plot, or prose, nor as he had thought, in the dramatic structure, but in half a dozen memorable tableaux, frozen moments of action, which are almostly certainly lifted from Walpole's dreams, and may be yours and mine, too."[11]

The inadequacy of the plot and structure is apparent, but we must not dismiss too quickly their overall effect in reinforcing the numinous element in the novel, namely, the struggle between what Otto would have called the "sacred" and the "profane." This conflict between two distinct ontological realities comes into focus in scenes in which the preternatural manifests itself. For example, Manfred, who is a kind of surrogate for the profane vision, finds himself struggling not so much against flesh and blood as against an epiphany of sacred entities which seek to frustrate his purpose. In the tableaus that dramatize this conflict—"frozen moments of action," in Wilt's phrase—natural objects are elevated to an animistic vision of the supernatural. The prosaic objects of everyday reality take on a surrealistic quality. This is evident in the scene in which Manfred, who seeks to put aside his wife Hippolita and marry Isabella, pursues Isabella into a chamber of the castle that serves as a portrait gallery:

> Manfred rose to pursue her; when the moon, which was now up and gleamed in at the opposite casement, presented to his sight the plumes of the fatal helmet, which rose to the height of the windows, waving backwards and forwards in a tempestuous manner, and accompanied with a hollow and rustling sound. . . . At that instant the portrait of his grandfather, which hung over the bench where they had been sitting, uttered a deep sigh and heaved its breast. . . . Manfred saw it quit its panel and descend [to] the floor with a grave and melancholy air.[12]

This sharply etched scene, reminiscent of Hamlet's encounter with his father's ghost, is a good example of Walpole's power to depict the "harmony of contrasts" in the numinous. The moon, gleaming through the casement and falling on the plumes of the "fatal helmet," suggests the contrasting qualities of awe and fascination. This "ideogram" (to use Otto's word) evokes the sense of *mysterium* at the same time that it hints of vague but powerful spiritual forces working against Manfred's dark—or "profane"— purpose. The note of wonder intensifies as the chamber is transformed into the haunted castle familiar in later Gothic literature. Manfred's determined efforts to resist or ignore the sacred epiphany now result in a second manifestation of the higher powers. The inanimate is transformed into the animate as the portrait of Manfred's grandfather utters a deep sigh and steps slowly and with dignity from its frame. At this point the note of *majestas* is dominant, trailing off into blank wonder as Manfred follows the wraith to the end of the chamber where the great door is shut with violence "as by an invisible hand."

Tableaus such as this tend to lift the story above its some-times turgid levels of dialogue and description. Not only do they impart a compelling sense of the uncanny to the novel, they invoke the "numinous value" Otto spoke of as well. If Manfred misses the implications of this ominous warning, the reader does not. By means of this numinous ideogram, Walpole suggests that vast, albeit hidden, powers are at work in the background, preserving the *sanctus*.

A similar but even more striking example of the numinous quality of the novel can be seen in a later tableau. Frederick, the Marquis of Vincenza, who has temporarily allied himself with Manfred's profane designs, enters a chapel within the castle grounds, where he comes upon a shrouded figure kneeling before an altar.

> The marquis, expecting the holy person to come forth, and meaning to excuse his uncivil interruption, said Reverend father, I sought the lady Hippolita.—Hippolita! replied a hollow voice; camest thou to this castle to seek Hippolita?— And then the figure, turning slowly round, discovered to Frederick the fleshless jaws and empty sockets of a skeleton, wrapt in a hermit's cowl. Angels of grace, protect me! cried Frederick recoiling.[13]

This, the first of many skeletal beings that populate Gothic fiction, attests to Walpole's ability to project numinous archetypes. The stark imagery of the passage is nevertheless latent with a strong sense of what Otto called the *mysterium,* the feeling of blank wonder called up by that which is "wholly other" and beyond all natural analogies. According to Otto, the true attraction of a ghost is that it is something that does not really exist in our scheme of reality. Also, one notes that Walpole has arranged the scene in such a way that it calls up distinct religious associations which contribute to the sense of sacred value.

This passage, I think, fully justifies a comment by Scott: "What is most striking in *The Castle of Otranto* is the manner in which the various prodigious appearances, bearing each upon the other, and all upon the accomplishment of the ancient prophecy, denouncing the ruin of the house of Manfred, gradually prepare us for the grand catastrophe."[14] This catastrophe, often praised by later critics, leans heavily on the numinous sense of *majestas:*

> A clap of thunder at that instant shook the castle to its foundations; the earth rocked, and the clank of more than mortal armour was heard behind. . . . [The] walls of the castle behind Manfred were thrown down with a mighty force, and the form of Alfonso, dilated to an immense magnitude, appeared in the centre of the ruins. . . . [It] ascended solemnly towards heaven, where the clouds parting asunder, the form of Saint Nicholas was seen; and receiving Alfonso's shade, they were soon wrapt from mortal eyes in a blaze of glory.[15]

This scene is perhaps a bit too theatrical for modern tastes, but it does elicit the sense of wonder and *majestas* to a degree quite beyond some of Walpole's later imitators. The various images—such as the supernatural clap of thunder, the clank of more than mortal armour, and the sudden demolition of the castle—lead up to the climactic image of the figure of Alfonso the Good, luminous in the clouds, as he enters heaven under the aegis of the gigantic figure of Saint Nicholas.

In this passage, and throughout the book, Walpole blends the sense of numinous wonder, the *mysterium,* with associations and images from medieval Catholicism. This was to become a standard feature of the Gothic novel, attesting to the integral association between the numinous and the religious instinct. That the conjunction of these two strains appeared at this stage of history is, as Eliade suggests, more than coincidence. The collapsing religious traditions of the period, coupled with the rise of a naked rationalism, drove many intellectuals to seek a deeper reality. In setting his novel in a background of medieval Catholicism, Walpole was instinctively responding to an emotional vacuum created by the demise of current religious traditions. As David Punter says in his *Literature of Terror,* Walpole originated "a genre in which the attractions of the past and of the supernatural become similarly connected, and further, in which the supernatural itself becomes a symbol of our past rising against us."[16] To have incorporated an archetypal vision of this nature into fiction is no small accomplishment. *The Castle of Otranto* rises above its occasional inadequacies and remains a benchmark in the history of the literature of the numinous.

Like all popular works, *The Castle of Otranto* inspired a host of imitators and resulted in the creation of a new genre: the Gothic novel. The setting of Walpole's book, its themes, and to some degree its action became stereotyped. If they were to succeed, all respectable Gothic novels had to show evidence of moldering castles, underground passages, clanking chains, and ghostly visitants. Once worked out, the formula became inflexible. The modern reader, surrounded by this "Gothic claptrap," can only wonder at the insatiable appetite of eighteenth-century readers for lore of this sort.

Amid this Gothic maze, some good work was produced, however. Some scholars—notably Montague Summers, Eino Railo, and Devendra Varma—have sifted through much of it, locating the valuable pieces for modern readers. The difficulty inherent in the Gothic novel lies in its overly intricate plotting, stilted dialogue, stereotyped characterization, and prolixity. Yet the reader who has learned to savor the numinous impulse that underlies much of this "Gothic welter" may find a peculiar pleasure in certain works not quite in the first rank. As in all major literary schools—whether the metaphysical, the Romantic, or the Symboliste—there are recurrent images and symbols, the recognition of which becomes fascinating. Railo has collected and sorted out much of this Gothic claptrap with an eye to discerning its part in the development of romanticism.[17]

Clara Reeve's *The Old English Baron* (1777) is a serviceable example of the uneven nature of much of this material.[18] Varma describes the book as "written in prudish objection to the free use of the supernatural in *The Castle of Otranto*."[19] In a preface to the novel, Mrs. Reeve described *Otranto* as too heavily laden with supernatural machinery. She sought to lessen the impact of ghostly elements by increasing what she called the book's "probability."[20] The ultimate effect is not always felicitious, however. Commenting on Mrs. Reeve's strategy, Walpole said: "I suppose the author thought a tame ghost might come within the laws of probability."[21] The ghosts in the book either come in dreams or are explained away by natural causes, which has the effect of making the numinous passages in the story seem merely superficial decorations. For example, when Edmund, the story's protagonist, enters the moldering, long deserted bedchamber beneath which the skeleton of his

dead father lies buried, the reader anticipates that an uncanny event is about to occur but, finding nothing of the
sort, feels he is being toyed with. "God defend us," said
Edmund,

> "but I verily believe that the person that owned this armor
> lies buried under us." Upon this, a dismal hollow groan was
> heard, as if from underneath. A solemn silence ensued, and
> marks of fear were visible upon all three; the groans were
> thrice heard. Oswald made signs for them to kneel, and he
> prayed audibly that Heaven would direct them how to act;
> he also prayed for the soul of the departed, that it might rest
> in peace. After this, he arose; but Edmund continued kneel-
> ing. He vowed solemnly to devote himself to the discovery
> of this secret, and then avenging the death of the person
> buried there.[22]

There are several effective, if stereotyped, elements in the
scene, including the inevitable guttering lamp, the portraits
of Edmund's dead parents with their faces turned toward
the wall, and the wind that shrieks intermittently about the
castle; but Mrs. Reeve dissipates their effect by her thoroughgoing rationalism. Edmund and his associates simply
discover the bloody suit of armor, pray in exemplary fashion,
and vow revenge. The ultimate effect is one of anticlimax,
leading the reader to suspect that Walpole was correct in
his somewhat ironic comment.[23] If one is going to have a
ghost, it should be one with some degree of ghostly élan
vital.

The vogue created by *Otranto* persisted through the last
quarter of the eighteenth-century, giving rise to a number of
novels which today are for the most part mercifully forgotten.
It was not until 1794 that a worthy successor to *Otranto*
appeared: Ann Radcliffe's *The Mysteries of Udolpho,* a
book which, despite numerous faults, has held its place as
one of the major Gothics.

Although Ann Radcliffe's strategy is similar to that of Clara Reeve's, her work is more successful. Like Reeve, she makes use of seemingly occult incidents which are explained away at the end of the story with an almost syllogistic logic. Admittedly, this tends to dissipate the very effect she is trying to create; but her instinctive feeling for the numinous triumphs over what, after all, would be an otherwise frivolous attempt to frighten the reader. By means of her superb ability to depict the sublime and her subtle rendering of what would appear to be the preternatural, she adumbrates the numinous reality that lies behind the world of everyday events.

Her use of the sublime, for example, is apparent in the novel's long opening section in which the heroine, Emily St. Aubert, accompanied by her father and her lover, Valancourt, journeys through the Pyrenees. A series of "terrific" incidents—including threats from banditti (ever present in the Gothic tradition), mysterious music heard at night, a haunted villa, and other indications of the occult—are combined with descriptions of the sublime mountain scenery through which the travelers pass:

> On the other side of the valley . . . a rocky pass opened toward Bascony. . . . Sometimes, indeed, a gigantic larch threw its long shade over the precipice, and here and there a cliff reared on its brow a monumental cross, to tell the traveller the fate of him who had ventured thither before . . . Soon after an object not less terrific struck her—a gibbet standing on a point of rock near the entrance of the pass, and immediately over one of the crosses she had before observed.[24]

Passages such as this indicate that Ann Radcliffe had read considerably in the eighteenth-century treatises on the Sublime. Edmund Burke, the most influential writer on the subject, had discussed sublimity as arising from astonishment, obscurity, power, privation, vastness, and infinity.[25] His ideas parallel those of Kant, Kames, Allison, and other writers on the subject.[26] The concept of sublimity, in fact, closely resembles the numinous, as Otto pointed out. "The analogies between the consciousness of the sublime and the numinous may be easily grasped," he wrote.

> To begin with, the "sublime," like the "numinous," is in Kantian language an idea or concept "that cannot be unfolded" or explicated (*unauswickelbar*). . . . A thing does not become sublime merely by being great. The concept itself remains unexplicated; it has in it something mysterious, and in this it is like the numinous. A second point of resemblance is that the sublime exhibits the same peculiar dual character as the numinous; it is at once daunting, and yet singularly attracting in its impress upon the mind. . . . so the idea of the sublime is closely similar to that of the numinous, and is well adapted to excite it and to be excited by it, while each tends to pass over into the other.[27]

The tendency for the sublime to "pass over" into the numinous is a favorite point with Otto:

> This mode of expression by way of grandeur or "sublimity" is found on higher levels, where it replaces mere "terror" or "dread." . . . While the element of "dread" is gradually overborne, the connection of "the sublime" and "the holy" becomes firmly established as a legitimate schematization and is carried on into the highest forms of religious consciousness.[28]

Analysis of the passage just cited suggests that Ann Radcliffe understood intuitively the connection between these two feeling-states, and that she used the sublime in nature to raise the mind to a sense of the numinous. The varied images of mountains, granite cliffs, barren hills, and clouds lead on to the image of the "monumental cross" on the brow of a cliff. This, in turn, is modified by a gathering sense of awe and mystery as Emily gazes upon "a gibbet standing on a point of a rock." Thus feelings associated with the sublime are gradually aroused, then abruptly transferred to a numinous ideogram—in this case, a cross with its associated religious implications. The numinous emotion thus aroused is modified at the end of the passage when both cross and gibbet appear fused in a *mysterium tremendum* that vibrates in the reader's mind.[29]

The use of this strategy—raising the sublime to the numinous—becomes almost explicit in Book II. In this much-praised section of the novel, Emily and her aunt, Madame Charon, are transported to the upper reaches of the Apennines by the villainous Montoni, who intends to hold them prisoner in his castle. The perils and uncertainties of the journey, alternating with descriptions of the mysteriously beautiful mountain scenery, blend to produce the sense of the sublime; and this, in turn, gives way to the sense of the numinous.

> At length the travellers began to ascend among the Apennines. The immense pine-forests . . . excluded all views but of the cliffs aspiring above, except that now and then, an opening through the dark woods allowed the eye a momentary glimpse of the country below. The gloom of these shades . . . assisted to raise the solemnity of Emily's feelings into awe; she saw only images of gloomy grandeur, or of dreadful sublimity around her; other images, equally gloomy and equally terrible, gleamed on her imagination.[30]

The imagery of the passage, based on the "ascent motif" already noted, serves to "raise the solemnity of Emily's feelings into awe." Similarly, the various artistic means for producing the numinous (obscurity, silence, darkness, intermittent light, empty distance) are called into play. The sense of awe increases as the travelers enter a deep valley and at last reach their goal: the castle of Udolpho.

> Emily gazed with melancholy awe upon the castle . . . for though it was lighted up by the setting sun, the gothic greatness of its features, and its mouldering walls of dark grey stone, rendered it a gloomy and sublime object. As she gazed, the light died away on its walls, leaving a melancholy purple tint, which spread deeper and deeper, as the thin vapour crept up the mountain, while the battlements above were still tipped with splendour. From these too, the rays soon faded, and the whole edifice was invested with the solemn duskiness of evening. Silent, lonely, and sublime, it seemed to stand the sovereign of the scene.[31]

Passages such as this make evident why the "haunted castle" was to become the unifying ideogram of Gothic literature, for this ideogram contains in essence that peculiar mixture of qualities Otto called the "harmony of contrasts" in the numinous. The darkness, silence, and sublimity of such structures, lit by an occasional glimmer of light, suggest by analogy the realm of existence that lies hidden behind the world of material reality. The association with medieval Catholicism adds to this sense of the ineffable. As in Otranto and Udolpho, each castle has its mysterious monks and nuns close at hand, a chapel with its guttering altar lamp, bleeding statues, and sonorous organ music. The religious associations blend with such numinous features as sullen moats, battlements, broken columns, winding archways, owls, ivy, and dark underground passages through which the terrified heroine escapes from her sinister pursuers. With their mixed "sacred and profane" symbolism, these castles acted as halfway houses between earth and heaven.

The haunted castle, in fact, is a fitting symbol for the concept Mircea Eliade calls "sacred space"—the numinous realm primitive man set aside for encounters with the *mys-*

terium. In the older religious view, Eliade says, space was not the homogeneous concept of modern "nonreligious man"; there were breaks and interruptions. Ordinary, or profane, space was contrasted with sacred space, which was strong and significant.[32] "Sacred space"—considered by religious man "the center of the world"—was often found on mountains or other high places.[33]

> As for the assimilation of temples to cosmic mountains and their function as links between earth and heaven, the names given to Babylonian sanctuaries themselves bear witness; they are called "Mountain of the House," "House of the Mountain of All Lands," "Mountain of Storms," "Link Between Heaven and Earth," and the like . . . Ascending is equivalent to an ecstatic journey to the center of the world; the pilgrim experiences a break-through from plane to plane; he enters a "pure region" transcending the profane world.[34]

In *The Mysteries of Udolpho* the feeling of sacred space blends with a sense of the preternatural, in accordance with Otto's ideas. Otto explains the magical or preternatural effect of Gothic architecture: "To us of the West the Gothic appears as the most numinous of all types of art. This is due in the first place to its sublimity . . . [but] the peculiar impressiveness of Gothic does not consist of its sublimity alone, but draws upon a strain inherited from primitive magic. . . ."[35]

The sense of magic and of the preternatural manifests itself within the castle. In addition to the various natural dangers that threaten her, Emily is surrounded by a series of occult phenomena: mysterious sounds, muffled voices, eerie whispers, strange yet beautiful music. On one occasion, lifting aside a black silk curtain, she gazes on a corpse wrapped in a winding sheet, the face partly eaten away by worms. Disoriented by these alien events, her mind is lifted to a perception of the numinous. As Radcliffe explains, "a terror of this nature, as it occupies and expands the mind, and elevates it to high expectation, is purely sublime, and leads us, by a kind of fascination, to seek even the object from which we appear to shrink."[36] This exposition of the "harmony of contrasts" is as clear as one could desire; it shows why Ann Radcliffe, more than any of her contemporaries, was able to create such striking images of the numinous. The numinous quality in her fiction is summed up by Varma:

> There is a mystic vagueness about the lovely landscape setting of Udolpho seen for the first time. Its gloom at nightfall, the ominous picture of its sombre exterior and shadow-haunted halls prepare us for the worst when we enter its portals. Our anticipation is a queer mixture of pleasure and fear, as we shudder at the impending events within its walls.[37]

If Ann Radcliffe is the master of the numinous "harmony of contrasts," Matthew Gregory Lewis, author of *The Monk* (1794), is her superior in depicting that peculiar aspect of the numinous Otto referred to as the "daemonic." This strange element in numinous feeling is explained by Otto as follows:

> In my examination of Wundt's *Animism,* I suggested the term Scheu (dread); but the special "numinous" quality (making it "awe" rather than "dread" in the ordinary sense) would then, of course, have to be denoted by the inverted commas. "Religious dread" (or "awe") would perhaps be a better designation. Its antecedent stage is "daemonic dread" (cf. the horror of Pan) with its queer perversion, a sort of abortive offshoot, the "dread of ghosts."[38]

Demons, gods, and other mythological conceptions spring from this root, as humanity has sought to embody such visions in concrete terms. The motif is prominent in Eastern religions, especially Mohammedanism, where wandering spirits (daemons), essentially "beyond good and evil," played a large part in primitive belief.[39] It is associated with Pan ("panic fear"), and Goethe, in a discussion with Eckhart, termed it "the daemonic."[40]

This murky and at times loathsome offshoot of numinous consciousness—which, as we will see, Otto described as the "negative numinous"—forms the core of Lewis's *The Monk*. In that strange and powerful novel Lewis pioneered the tale of damnation that influenced such later books as Maturin's *Melmoth the Wanderer*, Bram Stoker's *Dracula*, and the tales of Arthur Machen.[41] Here we have the numinous in its purely negative form, with all value elements reversed. The *tremendum* has become the merely daunting and horrifying, and the *sanctus* is twisted into the *profane*, producing a sense of sacrilege and evil that floods the mind with fear and loathing.

Like numerous other Gothic novels of the period, *The Monk* is an uneven book. Its formlessness, moral ambivalence, and occasional lapses of taste arise perhaps from the inexperience of its author, who was only twenty-one when he wrote it. As Edith Birkhead says, "the inflamed imagination, the violent exaggeration of emotion and character, the jeering cynicism, and the lack of tolerance, the incoherent formlessness, are all indications of adolescence."[42]

Despite these faults, *The Monk* has maintained a secure position among Gothic novels. John Berryman considers the central story, the section dealing with the monk Ambrosio, "passionate and astonishing. . . . Thomas Mann's *Doctor Faustus* seems to me frivolous by comparison."[43] For Devendra Varma, the book "remains a romance of extraordinary fascination and power."[44] For Eino Railo, it is "the highest and in many respects the most widely appreciated work of the terror-romanticism school," a judgment echoed by Montague Summers.[45] Classics succeed by exhibiting certain primary strengths rather than by displaying a lack of faults.

The basic power of *The Monk* lies in Lewis's ability to portray the daemonic element in the numinous by means of the occult tradition. This tradition—which evolved from gnosticism, medieval witchcraft, the kabbalah, and studies in the hermetic sciences—continues today in such mixed movements as anthrosophy, theosophy, spiritualism, and the Order of the Golden Dawn. Though apparently innocuous in certain forms (elements of so-called white magic, for example, appear in the writings of some of the early Scholastics), this tradition generally has tended toward an unhealthy interest in communication with the dead or with evil spirits.[46]

In *The Monk,* this daemonic strain appears in the sections dealing with Ambrosio, the monk of the title. Ambrosio is first shown as a severe, puritanical priest whose virtuous life and celebrated ability as a homilist have made him the cynosure of his order. Because of a pharisaic pride that underlies his character, combined with a hidden stream of passion, he is susceptible to the temptations of Matilda, a mysterious, evil woman who enters the monastery disguised as a monk. Having seduced Ambrosio, she proceeds to initiate him into the secrets of the occult.

The stages in this process of initiation are described by Lewis in horrifying detail. Having satisfied Ambrosio's lust for her, Matilda directs it toward Antonia, a beautiful young girl to whom Ambrosio acts as confessor. To obtain this prize, Matilda offers Ambrosio the aid of the Devil. When he hesitates, she shows him a magical mirror in which he sees the form of Antonia at her bath. Lust overpowers him, and, throwing the mirror down, he cries: "I yield, Matilda, I follow you. Do with me what you will."[47]

Accompanied by Ambrosio, Matilda descends into a labyrinthine cavern beneath the monastery for a meeting with the powers of evil. The details of this scene are so striking that, to savour the full sense of numinous horror, they should be read in their entirety. Leading Ambrosio into an enlarged portion of the cavern, Matilda temporarily leaves him beside a statue of Saint Clare, the patron of the order. During the interval, Ambrosio wavers between fear, despair, and hope. Darkness and strange sounds are all about him. He hears the voice of some tormented soul crying out: "God! Oh! God! No hope! No succour!"

Matilda returns at last, carrying a basket and a lamp. Leading Ambrosio farther along the passage, past graves, skulls and bones, she reaches another spot in the cavern, where she now performs the magic rituals traditionally used to invoke the powers of hell. These include the drawing of a protective circle and the chanting of incantations. Flames and smoke follow, then a mysterious glowing light, and at last the odor of perfume and the strains of sweet music. "He comes!" Matilda exclaims, and the demon appears. Expecting to see some horrible apparition, Ambrosio is surprised to witness the comely figure of a naked youth. "His form shone with dazzling glory; he was surrounded by clouds of rose-coloured light, and at the moment that he appeared, a refreshing air breathed perfumes through the cavern." Despite this ethereal beauty, Ambrosio remarks "a wildness in the daemon's eyes, and a mysterious melancholy impressed upon his features, betraying the fallen angel, and inspiring the spectators with secret awe."

The interview is successful, and the apparition vanishes, leaving the traditional myrtle branch with Matilda as a token of his fealty. "I have succeeded," she tells Ambrosio, "though with more difficulty than I expected. Lucifer, whom I summoned to my assistance, was at first unwilling to obey my commands. . . . I was constrained to have recourse to my strongest charms."

Unaware of the collusion of evil against him, Ambrosio
sets out upon a course of destruction which involves him in
a series of depradations that includes murder and rape. The
progress of his damnation is slow but inexorable. When he
is finally discovered and falls into the hands of the Inquisition, he again seeks help from the powers of hell. This
time, however, the fiend appears in a different guise.

> But he came not as when at Matilda's summons he borrowed
> the seraph's form to deceive Ambrosio. He appeared in all
> that ugliness which since his fall from heaven had been his
> portion. His blasted limbs still bore the marks of the Al-
> mighty's thunder. A swarthy darkness spread itself over his
> gigantic form; his hands and feet were armed with long
> talons. Fury glared in his eyes.[48]

In desperation Ambrosio agrees to the satanic bargain but
is subsequently tricked by the fiend, who takes him to a
great height and sends him plunging to the earth where he
lies in terrible suffering for six days before death mercifully
overtakes him.[49]

In the "daemonic" scenes discussed here, Lewis added
a new and disturbing dimension to the Gothic tradition.[50]
The feeling of profanity, or "negative numinous," that pervades the Ambrosio sections lifts the book above many of
its contemporaries. The firmness and subtlety with which
Lewis develops his dark theme render the book impregnable
to the faint sense of irony that modern readers sometimes
feel toward the Gothic.

Succeeding generations of writers have, in fact, felt the
influence of Lewis's genius. One such writer was Charles
Robert Maturin (1780–1830), whose remarkable if flawed
masterpiece *Melmoth the Wanderer* (1820) captures much
of the feeling of the daemonic in its central character. Mel-

moth the Wanderer, prototype of the Wandering Jew, has committed some unspecified sin of intellectual pride. As a result he is doomed to wander the earth for a period of 150 years or until he finds some mortal who will assume his burden in exchange for riches and supernatural power. To find such a victim, Melmoth seeks out individuals in various extremes of suffering and discomfort. In each instance Melmoth appears under mysterious circumstances and makes his proposal. The list of human sufferers includes an Englishman fraudulently confined to a madhouse, a Spanish youth forced to enter a monastery, and a father whose impoverished family is starving before his eyes. Thus the novel becomes in reality a series of individual narratives linked together by the central figure of Melmoth.

This structure provides a broad canvas for Maturin's powerful, realistic imagination. The slightly shopworn furniture of Gothicism—storms and shipwrecks, dungeons and subterranean vaults, graveyards, the horrors of the Inquisition, and all manner of preternatural events—takes on a new, rich life under Maturin's genius.[51] Moreover, in the character of Melmoth, Maturin fashioned an archetype that reminds one, to some degree, of Otto's description of the "urgency" or "energy" in the numinous object:

The figure stood at the door for some time, and then advancing slowly till it gained the centre of the room, it remained there fixed for some time, but without looking at them . . . —it was indeed Melmoth the Wanderer. . . .

The Wanderer waved his arm with an action that spoke defiance without hostility—and the strange and solemn accents of the only human voice that had respired mortal air beyond the period of mortal life, and never spoke but to the ear of guilt or suffering, and never uttered to that ear aught but despair, rolled slowly on their hearing like a peal of distant thunder.[52]

The portrait of the Wanderer, with its mixture of preternatural power and hopeless despair, echoes through many later daemonic characters, including Emily Brontë's Heathcliff, Melville's mad Captain Ahab, and Bram Stoker's Dracula. Maturin's genius is of that dark, almost existential kind favored by modern readers.[53] There can be no doubt that the book deserves the high reputation it has achieved over the years.[54]

Despite its evident strengths, however, I am forced to admit that the numinous element in the book is of a very uneven nature. For example, the frame structure, with its arrangement of a-tale-within-a-tale, dissipates the sustained building of numinous feeling. The cameo appearances of the Wanderer in each narrative become repetitious, lessening the sense of mystery and wonder. Eventually the reader comes to anticipate each tale's climax, knowing full well that Melmoth will appear to the sufferer, propose his bargain, and find himself rejected.

> "You need not guess," said Walberg, interrupting her. "I will tell you all. . . . Every night since our late distresses, I have wandered out in search of some relief, and supplicated every passing stranger;—latterly, I have met every night the enemy of man. . . ."
>
> "And in what form does he appear?" said Ines.
>
> "In that of a middle-aged man, of a serious and staid demeanour, and with nothing remarkable in his aspect except the light of two burning eyes, whose lustre is almost intolerable. . . . He has offered, and proved to me, that it is in his power to bestow all that human cupidity could thirst for, on the condition that—I cannot utter! It is one so full of horror and impiety, that, even to listen to it, is scarce less a crime than to comply with it!"[55]

Scenes like this, constantly repeated in one form or another, reinforce the didactic purpose spelled out in the book's preface: to prove that no human being, despite all possible temptations, would consciously barter away his soul. Such a didactic purpose, which would be unobjectionable in certain writing genres, at last becomes obtrusive in *Melmoth the Wanderer*. Melmoth's mysterious and bitter irony, his implacable hatred, and his numinous powers seem after a while slightly theatrical. By the end of the story he seems almost an allegorical figure. The numinous elements in the book take on an artificial quality and are ultimately "rationalized" by the consciously moralistic structure. To use the concepts of Rudolf Otto, one might say that the nonrational factors in the story are at odds with the rational factors. Thus, despite Maturin's indisputable power and originality, the reader may experience an unintentional irony in *Melmoth the Wanderer*, summed up perhaps in a remark by Poe: "He [Melmoth] labors indefatigably, through three octave volumes to accomplish the destruction of two or three souls, while any common devil would have demolished one or two thousand."[56]

Melmoth the Wanderer, the last of the "classical" Gothics, sums up many of the strengths and weaknesses of the tradition.[57] The various elements of Gothicism, brought together by Walpole and the other writers discussed in this chapter, were merged into the general stream of Romantic fiction as seen in the novels of James Hogg, Sir Walter Scott, the Brontës, and later in Wilkie Collins and Charles Dickens. In such works the numinous is often eliminated entirely, or it becomes a peripheral element.

In the work of other writers, the numinous impulse continued undiminished. I shall attempt in the succeeding chapters of this book to analyze a few such writers who are representative of this peculiar category of experience.

4

Frankenstein

A curious feature of many supernatural tales—one already remarked on—is their apparent lack of clear, distinct moral values. Often in such tales, the person who encounters the supernatural agent appears to do so by the merest chance and without conscious choice. The protagonist seems inadvertently to have crossed an invisible boundary or terminus, and in consequence he finds himself involved in a confrontation with supernatural reality. Because choices are not involved, these stories often appear to lack moral content; yet the reader often feels that some obscure value elements are present.

A brief example should clarify this point. In M. R. James's classic ghost story, "Oh, Whistle and I'll Come to You My Lad," a mild-mannered, innocuous professor named Parkins, on a golfing holiday in East Anglia, stumbles by chance upon an ancient, long-buried preceptory that had once belonged to the medieval Order of Templars. Poking about the ruins, Parkins discovers an old pipe or whistle, which he carries back to his hotel. Out of mere curiosity, he cleans the pipe off, instinctively puts it to his lips, and blows a few notes.

Throughout the story, Parkins is depicted as a thoroughly upright, decent individual. His main characteristic is a certain skepticism with regard to the preternatural. Although this is not depicted as a moral fault, the thrust of the story is to show the inadequacy of this view and the difficulties that can arise from it. Parkins is warned by a friend who has some experience with the occult that such objects as the whistle may be a source of danger—a warning Parkins ignores—with the result that he summons up (or "whistles up") a particularly loathsome, preternatural visitant from whom he escapes only with great difficulty. The ultimate effect of this incident is to produce in Parkins a new and rather humble respect for things that lie "beyond mortal ken."

The interesting feature of "Oh, Whistle" is that, while no ethical questions in the usual sense are raised, certain indistinct value elements do seem to be present. For instance, in the course of the narrative, Parkins's attitude changes from one of skepticism toward the unseen to one approximating belief, as though the author were issuing vague warnings against Parkins's rigid positivism. And, whereas the events of the story obviously are fictional, the reader experiences a faint recognition of a reality lurking in the background.

The problem is that the moral factors involved in such stories seem to bear little relation to the usual "rational" values one finds in such writers as George Eliot, Thackeray, Flaubert, and other realists. In fact, to the degree that modern critics have paid any attention at all to supernatural literature, the question of its moral value has been a troubling one. Later, when studying the work of Edgar Allan Poe, we will find that one of the major charges brought against his work is that it is "morally empty." Indeed, the modern critical school, while fully equipped to deal with extremely subtle and unconventional values, is not prepared to analyze values that lie beyond the rational. Even Freudian analysis fails at this point, as one can discover by reading Freud's essay "The Uncanny," in which he argues that supernatural fear arises from fear of the dead.[1] It might just as reasonably be argued that fear of the dead—the most harmless of creatures—arises from fear of the supernatural.

The problem of axiological, or moral, elements in numinous literature becomes crucial in the work we next turn to: Mary Shelley's *Frankenstein* (1818). On the surface *Frankenstein* seems to offer a series of typical nineteenth-century romantic values, values derived from the author's unconventional, revolutionary philosophy.[2] A closer reading, however, suggests that these supposed values are contradicted by the main events of the novel.

The Romantic values are voiced by Victor Frankenstein himself in a number of places, as well as by the monster he creates. In long declamatory passages he expounds on such themes as the injustice of society, the inequality of wealth, and the need for change. It appears at times that Mary Shelley is merely expressing the radical philosophy she absorbed from her father William Godwin and her husband Percy Bysshe Shelley. Frankenstein, an advocate of science and progress, hopes to alleviate the ills of mankind by making a momentous scientific discovery. The monster, sounding at times like a disciple of Rousseau, sets forth with utopian bombast the possibilities of a good society, if only the conventional "evils" of mankind can be eliminated. Superstition, ignorance, intolerance, and inequality seem to be the targets of this typical nineteenth-century protest.[3]

When we take a closer look, however, we find an underlying conflict between the rhetoric of the book and the events of the story. In his enthusiasm for science and his utopian desire to aid humanity, Frankenstein thinks of himself as a benefactor of mankind. He feels no compunction as he conducts the gruesome task of collecting parts for the monster's body, then animating his creation. No sooner does the monster take its first breath than Frankenstein feels a sense of moral revulsion toward the creature. He feels loathing and disgust for the monster, an antipathy that increases as the story continues. Frankenstein views the ill fortune that dogs his steps through the novel as retribution for his act of creation. "I felt," he says, "as if I had committed some great crime, the consciousness of which haunted me. I was guiltless, but I had indeed drawn down a horrible curse upon my head, mortal as that of crime."[4]

This ambiguous note extends to the monster. At one moment spouting utopian fustian, while at the next, committing horrifying atrocities, he suggests a degree of moral ambivalence, as though Mary Shelley were not certain of the idea she wished to convey. Such moral puzzles have been largely ignored by critics, due, not doubt, to the novel's massive power and psychological momentum.[5] Anyone reading it for the first time will almost certainly be swept forward by its thrilling incidents, originality of conception, and profound numinous impulse. Its young author created a group of archetypes that have fascinated people for a century and a half and that will almost certainly continue to fascinate future generations. In other words, despite its apparent moral ambivalence, the novel contains a profound sense of underlying moral unity.[6]

It is at this point, and in search of answers to this problem, that we return briefly to Otto's ideas on numinous values. The subject is discussed in a chapter from *The Idea of the Holy* entitled "The Holy as a Category of Value." The numinous, Otto reminds his reader, begins as a sense of "creature-feeling" that the percipient experiences when encountering *the sacred*. This "creature-feeling' is described as a sense of "dis-valuation" before that which is infinitely superior to the percipient. As examples of this phenomenon, Otto cites passages from the Bible. In the *Old*

Testament is found Isaiah's cry: "I am a man of *unclean* lips and dwell among a people of unclean lips"; and from the *New Testament,* Peter's exclamation to Jesus: "Depart from me, for I am a *sinful* man, Oh Lord." In both instances, Otto contends, the feeling response

> is not based on deliberation, nor does it follow any rule, but breaks . . . palpitant from the soul—like a direct reflex movement at the stimulation of the numinous. It does not spring from the consciousness of some committed transgression, but rather is an immediate datum given with the feeling of the numen; it proceeds to "disvalue" together with the self, the tribe to which the person belongs, and indeed, together with that, all existence in general.[7]

This feeling of "dis-valuation" is not based on a sense of personal wrongdoing but rather on a sense of one's *profaneness.* The individual's very existence as a creature is "disvalued" before the absolute value of the numen. Accompanying the sense of dis-valuation, however, is another feeling, one centered on the numinous object itself. This is a sense of appreciation of the value of the numinous object: "a unique kind of category diametrically contrary to 'the profane,' the category of 'the holy' which is proper to the numen alone, but to it in an absolute degree." To this numinous object the traditional response has always been, "Tu solus sanctus." The *sanctus* is not merely "perfect" or "beautiful" or "sublime" or "good"; rather, "it is the positive numinous value or worth, and to it corresponds on the side of the creature a numinous disvalue or 'unworth.' "[8]

Proper terms for this sense of supreme valuation are the Greek σεμνός and the Latin *augustus.* The sense of numinous value and its corresponding sense of disvalue are especially prominent in the more primitive religions of mankind, but the feeling has not disappeared altogether from the more advanced religions. As the feeling develops, it partakes of moral categories, yet retains its autonomous character. The fully developed concept of "sin," in fact, emerges only when the feeling of numinous disvalue is transferred to and centered in moral delinquency. In his later *Religious Essays,* Otto clarified this idea to some extent:

> In the beginning, sin lies in an entirely different realm from the bad. In the early stages of the development of these ideas, sin and the religious "impurity" which result from it need not invade moral values in the least, and may yet lie with terrible weight upon the spirit. . . . In its essence it is a negligent or intentional slight to a numinous object—of whatever kind; and in this sense it is a violation of the unique objective value of the *august* or σεμνός in any of its manifestations.[9]

Whatever theoretical objections might be raised against Otto's theory of numinous value, its phenomenological reality seems beyond question, as evidenced by many examples from anthropology and religious history. One well-known authority in the field of religious history, R. R. Marett, has studied a similar phenomenon among natives of the Pacific Islands, and concludes that

> Science, then, may adopt *mana* as a general category to designate the positive aspect of the supernatural, or sacred, or whatever we are to call that order of miraculous happenings which, for the concrete experience, if not usually for the abstract thought of the savage, is marked off perceptibly from the order of ordinary happenings. *Tabu,* on the other hand, may serve to designate its negative aspect. That is to say, negatively, the supernatural is *tabu,* not lightly approached, because positively, it is *mana,* instinct with power above the ordinary.[10]

With Otto's concept of numinous value in mind, we now turn to Mary Shelley's *Frankenstein* and attempt to analyze the peculiar moral problem discussed earlier. I shall try to show that Mary Shelley uses the concepts of the sacred and the profane to repudiate a central myth of the nineteenth century: the all-sufficiency of man when he cuts himself loose from tradition and relies on science and raw rationality. *Frankenstein* was one of the first works to dramatize this theme.

Like many of his later progeny, Frankenstein is perhaps the first of many "mad scientists" in literature—men who look for salvation to the sheerly rational (in Otto's sense of the term). Thus he is quite similar to what Eliade calls "desacralized" man. According to Eliade, the universe of modern man has lost its cosmological significance. It is opaque, inert, mute: "it transmits no message, it holds no cipher."[11] In like manner, modern "nonreligious" man's body has lost all spiritual significance. External nature as well as human nature has been progressively secularized, the result being what Eliade views as "profane man." To acquire power and control, modern man has "desacralized the world in which his ancestors lived."[12]

This process of desacralization is clearly depicted in the early chapters of the novel, where we see the youthful protagonist, Victor Frankenstein, set out on the somewhat callow pursuit of "the mysteries of heaven and earth."[13] Encountering the writings of Cornelius Agrippa, Paracelsus, and Albertus Magnus, he is led into a search for the philosophers' stone and the elixir of life. Pursuit of these spurious goals (Frankenstein later calls them "chimeras") is undertaken with worthy motives: Frankenstein hopes to "banish disease from the human frame, and render man invulnerable to any but a violent death."[14] One cannot help noting a certain rash, even profane, quality about his early aspirations. For example, the writers who influence Frankenstein in his course of study were, with the exception of Albertus Magnus, sixteenth- and seventeenth-century pseudo-scientists who today are regarded as charlatans. Relying on a methodology that was half-scientific, half-occult, they sought to acquire by profane means a knowledge traditionally considered the domain of religion. Like the older Gnostics and alchemists, they pursued goals which, if successful, would have revealed the forbidden secrets of life itself.

The role of these pseudo-scientists is commented on by C. S. Lewis in a passage that throws light on *Frankenstein:*

> I have described as a "magician's bargain" that process whereby man surrenders object after object, and finally himself, to Nature in return for power. And I meant what I said. The fact that the scientist has succeeded where the magician failed has put such a wide contrast between them in popular thought that the real story of the birth of Science is misunderstood. . . . The serious magical endeavor and the serious scientific endeavor are twins: one was sickly and died, the other strong and throve. But they were twins. They were born of the same impulse. . . . In Paracelsus the characters of magician and scientist are combined. No doubt those who really founded modern science were usually those whose love of truth exceeded their love of power; in every mixed movement the efficacy comes from the good elements, not from the bad. But the presence of the bad elements is not irrelevant to the direction the efficacy takes. It might be going too far to say that the modern scientific movement was tainted from its birth; but I think it would be true to say that it was born in an unhealthy neighborhood and at an inauspicious hour. Its triumphs may have been too rapid and purchased at too high a price. . . .[15]

Whether or not one agrees entirely with Lewis, it seems clear that his interpretation of the origin of modern science finds an embodiment in *Frankenstein.* In the portion of the novel that takes place at the University of Ingoldstadt, Frankenstein comes to realize that he can attain his goal of discovering the intimate secrets of life only by a more practical methodology. Two of his professors at the university, Kempe and Waldemar, assure him that the fantastic speculations of Agrippa and Paracelsus are worthless but that the goal of power can be attained by patient study, hard work, and an empirical approach to science. "The modern masters," Waldemar tells him, "promise very little. They know that metals cannot be transmuted, and that the elixir of life is a chimera. But these philosophers, whose hands seem only made to dabble in dirt, and their eyes to pore over the microscope or crucible, have indeed performed miracles. . . . They have acquired new and almost unlimited power."[16] These words kindle in Victor Frankenstein a wild ambition. He will combine the goals of the magician with the methods of science. Such a goal is not evil in the conventional sense of the word; rather, it is profane. Frankenstein's limited view of reality leads him to undertake a truncated form of creation that parodies the sacred.

As the subtitle of the book suggests, Frankenstein is "the modern Prometheus." Obviously, however, the version of the myth Mary Shelley has in mind is not that of Prometheus the fire-bringer but rather Prometheus *plasticator,* in which the Titan is the creator of mankind.[17] The epigraph from *Paradise Lost* reinforces this idea. The words of Adam— "Did I request thee, Maker, from my clay to mould me man?"—hint that Frankenstein is to be thought of as a creator, but a creator-manqué. His creation, devoid of sacred significance, is at one with the desacralizing tendency Eliade attributes to modern post-religious man.

The profanity of this creation is hinted at in the account of Frankenstein's discovery of the principle of animation.[18] "To examine the causes of life," he says,

> we must first have recourse to death. . . . In my education my father had taken the greatest precautions that my mind should be impressed with no supernatural horrors. I do not ever remember to have trembled at a tale of superstition, or to have feared the apparition of a spirit. Darkness had no effect upon my fancy and a churchyard was to me merely the receptacle of bodies deprived of life.

Since all feeling for the numinous and the sacred was deliberately omitted from his childhood experience, his conception of life and death is purely scientific and rational. The sacred mysteries of existence—frightening in some aspects but also ennobling—are beyond his interest. "Now I was led to examine the cause and progress of this decay, and forced to spend days and nights in vaults and charnel houses. My attention was fixed upon every object the most insupportable to the delicacy of human feelings."[19]

Although at the time filled with "delight and rapture," Frankenstein learns in retrospect that some essential element of human nature was missing from his strange preoccupation. He cautions his auditor: "Learn from me . . . how dangerous is the acquirement of knowledge and how much happier that man is who believes his native town to be the world than he who aspires to become greater than his nature will allow."

Realization of the profanity of his experiments has come to him in later years. He speaks of it as an "employment loathsome in itself, but which had taken an irresistible hold of my imagination." The quest had "swallowed up every habit of my nature." In fact, as the account of his creation continues, his vocabulary begins to echo the sacred-profane terminology used by Otto:

> who shall conceive the horrors of my secret toil as I dabbled among the unhallowed damps of the grave and tortured the living animal to animate the lifeless clay? . . . I collected bones from charnel houses and disturbed with profane fingers the tremendous secrets of the human frame. In a solitary chamber, or rather cell, at the top of the house . . . I kept my workshop of filthy creation.

The sense of revulsion that Frankenstein experiences as his work continues reaches a climax in the scene where he succeeds in animating the monster. In this instance—and, indeed, in every sequence in which the monster appears—

Mary Shelley suggests the sacred-profane theme by means of a recurring symbol pattern in which the beautiful is contrasted with the ugly and the real with the counterfeit. Particular symbols within the pattern are the moon, water, inclement weather, and a series of natural objects which might otherwise be beautiful but are rendered repulsive by the pale, sickly hues in which they are described:

> It was on a dreary night of November that I beheld the accomplishment of my toils. . . . It was already one in the morning; the rain pattered dismally against the panes, and my candle was nearly burnt out, when, by the glimmer of the half-extinguished light, I saw the dull yellow eye of the creature open; it breathed hard, and a convulsive motion agitated its limbs.
>
> How can I describe my emotions at this catastrophe, or how delineate the wretch whom with such infinite pains and care I had endeavoured to form? His limbs were in proportion and I had selected his features as beautiful. Beautiful— Great God! His yellow skin scarcely covered the work of muscles and arteries beneath; his hair was a lustrous black, and flowing; his teeth of a pearly whiteness; but these luxuriances only formed a more horrid contrast with his watery eyes, that seemed almost of the same colour as the dun white sockets in which they were set, his shrivelled complexion and straight black lips.

At this point Frankenstein fully realizes the unhallowed nature of his creation. "Now that I had finished," he says, "the beauty of the dream vanished and breathless horror and disgust filled my heart." Rushing from the laboratory and into his bedchamber, he falls into a fitful sleep, only to be awakened by the cold touch of the creature's hand. At this point, the "dim and yellow light of the moon" enters the chamber and Frankenstein sees "the wretch—the miserable monster whom I had created." The thing opens its jaws and murmurs inarticulately; "a grin wrinkled his cheeks." Frankenstein flees into the night and wanders about as a cold rain falls on him. Finally, as the wet dawn breaks, he sees "the church of Ingoldstadt, its white steeple and clock, which indicated the sixth hour."

In these passages we see symbolic associations with the theme of the sacred versus the profane. The monster's features, though individually beautiful, are hideous when taken as a whole. His eyes—"pale yellow" and "watery"—are associated with the "dim yellow light of the moon" and the cold rain that beats on the window. The moon, a sort of "lesser light of creation," is in fact symbolically a simulacrum of the sun, just as the monster is a counterfeit of true life. Frankenstein has violated the sacred nature of reality, and in consequence his creation breathes an eerie quality of unreality: pale colors, moonlight, water. The effect is reinforced by the monster's inarticulate murmurs, his blundering movements and wrinkled grin—a parody of a true smile.

These symbolic associations with the sacred and the profane cast light on Frankenstein's violent alteration of feeling. In *Mary Shelley's Frankenstein,* Christopher Small comments on the question without solving it. "There is a problem here," he states,

> proverbially described but not elucidated: why should good intentions lead to hell? Neither the moral schemes of Godwin or Milton can solve it. . . . Mary Shelley did not solve it either, for it is, of course, the sort of puzzle incapable of solution by any formula. . . . Mary introduced what looks like a moral confusion.[20]

The problem stated by Small is not, however, insoluble.[21] The supposed moral confusion disappears in the light of Rudolf Otto's theory of sacred and profane values. Although

Frankenstein begins his quest for the mystery of life from the highest motives, he now acts without regard for sacred reality. He has short-circuited the divine creativity. Looking back at the train of circumstances that led to the creation of the monster, he says: "I wished to procrastinate . . . all that related to my feelings of affection until the great object, which swallowed up every habit of my nature, should be completed."[22] The quest for a wholly rational object, pursued without the mediating influence of the affections or a sense of the sacred, has resulted in *the profane.* He has slighted the numinous object and plunged into an abyss of mere duration. In this regard there is perhaps a touch of symbolism in the description of the steeple and clock that Frankenstein sees on the morning after his experiment: the clock suggesting the endless, empty profanity of mere time and the church steeple throwing up visions of the sacred.

Thus, despite his later denials of guilt, one must not assume that Frankenstein is blameless. Although he has not consciously transgressed a moral law, he nevertheless has violated the sacred values that cluster about the numinous object.[23] The conquest of nature has been achieved at too high a cost. As Eliade puts it:

> The reader will very soon realize that sacred and profane are two modes of being in the world, two existential situations assumed by man in the course of history. . . . In the last analysis, the sacred and profane modes of being depend upon different positions that man has conquered in the cosmos. . . .[24]

In the remainder of the novel Mary Shelley shows the result of this initial act of sacrilege working itself out in reality. Following his experiments in creating the monster, Frankenstein undergoes a mental breakdown. Later, upon returning to his home in Geneva, he learns of the murder of his younger brother and is convinced that the monster is the murderer. In an attempt to compose himself, he takes a trip into the Alps and there once again confronts the monster, who has been living in a small hut.

The crucial tenth chapter of the novel, which describes this meeting, is of particular importance from our viewpoint, in that it represents a kind of microcosm of the numinous impulse of the story. In the region of the Montavert Glacier and within the shadow of Mont Blanc, Frankenstein begins his ascent. The magnificent scenery around him, sublime yet barren, enhances the sense of *mysterium tremendum.* "It is a scene terrifically desolate. In a thousand spots the traces of the winter avalanche may be perceived, where trees lie broken and strewed on the ground, some entirely destroyed, others bent, leaning upon the jutting rocks of the mountain or transversely upon other trees."[25] As he reaches the ice field, "rising like the waves of a troubled sea," a mist descends. Looking upon this alien yet beautiful scene, Frankenstein experiences the sense of *fascinans:* "My heart, which was before sorrowful, now swelled with something like joy; I exclaimed—'Wandering spirits, if indeed ye wander, and do not rest in your narrow beds, allow me this faint happiness, or take me, as your companion, away from the joys of life.' " The enrapt sense of *presence* is abruptly dissipated when Frankenstein spies the huge shape of the monster bounding toward him across the glacier. The vision produces in him that sensation which Otto might describe as *stupor* ("I was troubled; a mist came over my eyes, and I felt a faintness seize me"). The awesome, daunting notes of the numinous are now uppermost.

> I perceived, as the shape came nearer (sight tremendous and abhorred?) that it was the wretch whom I had created. . . . He approached; his countenance bespoke bitter anguish, combined with disdain and malignity, while its unearthly ugliness rendered it almost too horrible for human eyes.

At this point, the contrast between sacred and profane reaches a climax. The unearthly beauty of the mountains, the barrenness of broken trees and rocks, and the alien quality of the frozen glacier set into faint vibration the *harmony of contrasts* in the numinous. This in turn is contrasted with the preternatural ugliness and horror of the monster, producing the sense of profanity that Otto termed "the negative numinous."

In the encounter between Frankenstein and the monster that follows, Mary Shelley intensifies the contrast by evoking a feeling of partial sympathy for the monster. As he describes to Frankenstein his wanderings and misadventures in the world of mankind, the monster projects a sense of his humanity but of a weird, blighted kind. Hounded by all who have seen him, an object of fear and loathing, he has come to hate all mankind; but he hastens to add that he is still capable of goodness: "I was benevolent and good; misery made me a fiend. Make me happy, and I shall again be virtuous."

Some have seen the monster's words as constituting the moral center of the novel. One of these readers was Mary's husband Percy Bysshe Shelley, who summed up his view thus: "Treat a person ill and he will become wicked."[26] As I have suggested, however, the moral implications of the novel seem far less simplistic than this interpretation would indicate. First, the supposed benevolence of the monster is far from clear. In this, as well as later scenes, Mary Shelley suggests a note of sly malignity about the monster which belies his idealistic words. His face, we are told, displays "bitter anguish, combined with disdain and malignity." His "ghastly grin," the subtlety of his speech, and the unearthly rages of which he is capable ("his face was wrinkled into contortions too horrible for human eyes to behold") suggest a sinister quality. Even on the several occasions when Frankenstein is moved by pity, he still feels distrust.

Second, and more to the point, the monster evokes from everyone he encounters the feeling of *mysterium* combined with a sense of horror. "I compassioned him," Frankenstein says, "and sometimes felt a wish to console him; but when I looked upon him, when I saw the filthy mass that moved and talked, my heart sickened, and my feelings were altered to those of horror and hatred."[27] A nebulous sense of evil (the negative numinous), along with the feeling of the uncanny, places the monster beyond the reach of human sympathy.

There is no imaginable way, the reader feels, that the monster can be integrated into society, no matter how well treated. The implications of Percy Bysshe Shelley's comment lead only to a sense of the ludicrous. By his original act of sacrilege, even if it was not wholly intentional, Frankenstein has produced a nightmare that must be destroyed.

As a result of their meeting, the monster extorts from Frankenstein a promise to create a mate for him. To carry out this second "creation," Frankenstein moves to a remote island in the Orkneys. The bleak, barren landscape of the scene forms a proper numinous background for the task at hand. "It was a place fitted for such work," he says, "being hardly more than a rock, whose high sides were continually beaten upon by the waves. The soil was barren. . . . On the whole island there were but three miserable huts, and one of these was vacant when I arrived."

In one of these isolated cottages on the island, Frankenstein assembles his equipment and starts to work. As he proceeds, however, growing doubts intrude upon him, for this time he is at least partially aware of the profane implications of his task. "It was indeed a filthy process in which I was engaged. During my first experiment, a kind of enthusiastic frenzy had blinded me to the horror of my employment. . . . But now I went to it in cold blood, and my heart often sickened at the work of my hands."

On the night in which his work is completed, Frankenstein becomes fully aware of the sacrilege he is repeating when the monster himself arrives at his cottage and peers at him through the window. The description of this frightening scene makes use of the sacred-profane symbolism already noted, with the moon—symbol of the false act of creation—especially prominent. "I trembled and my heart failed within me when, looking up, I saw, by the light of the moon, the demon at the casement. A ghastly grin wrinkled his lips as he gazed on me."

Frankenstein resolves not to repeat his mistake. "I thought with a sensation of madness of my promise of creating another like to him, and trembling with passion, tore to pieces the thing on which I was engaged. The wretch saw me destroy the creature . . . and, with a howl of devilish despair and revenge, withdrew." The following night, under a pale moon, Frankenstein sinks his equipment and the remains of this second creation in the sea. Meanwhile the monster visits him again, and, after flying into a rage, promises revenge: "I shall be with you on your wedding-night."

The promise is soon redeemed. Frankenstein journeys to Italy, where the monster, true to his word, joins him, and on Frankenstein's wedding night, murders his bride.

The murderous mark of the fiend's grasp was on her neck, and the breath had ceased to issue from her lips. . . . While I still hung over her in the agony of despair, I happened to look up. The windows of the room had before been darkened, and I felt a kind of panic on seeing the pale yellow light of the moon illuminate the chamber. The shutters had been thrown back; and, with a sensation of horror not to be described, I saw at the open window a figure the most hideous and abhorred. A grin was on the face of the monster; he seemed to jeer, as with his fiendish finger he pointed towards the corpse of my wife.

The recurrent pattern of symbols (sacred versus profane) is used one last time. A few weeks later, Frankenstein goes to a nearby graveyard to mourn his lost bride. He vows to destroy the creature but is suddenly disturbed by a fiendish laugh that rings out. "I darted toward the spot from which the sound proceeded, but the devil eluded my grasp. Suddenly the broad disk of the moon arose and shone full upon his ghastly and distorted shape as he fled with more than mortal speed."

The final scenes of the book, chronicling Frankenstein's pursuit of the monster, serve as a numinous coda to the preceding strange events. Deliberately leaving a trail behind him, the monster heads north, followed by his obsessed creator. "Amidst the wilds of Tartary and Russia, although he still evaded me, I have ever followed in his track. . . . The snows descended on my head, and I saw the print of the huge step on the white plain." As Frankenstein and the monster move north into the polar region, the scenery becomes wilder, reinforcing the element of *mysterium:* "Immense and rugged mountains of ice often barred up my passage, and I often heard the thunder of the sea."[28] Frankenstein catches intermittent glimpses of the monster, who nevertheless manages to elude him every time. At last, almost dead from exhaustion, Frankenstein is taken aboard a ship chartered by a Captain Walton, who is exploring the region. Frankenstein relates his strange tale to Walton, then dies. In the final scene, the monster enters the cabin of the ship, mourns his dead creator, and departs, telling Walton that he intends to immolate himself in a funeral pyre.

Thus the story is resolved in the only feasible way: both the creator and the creation perish. The profanity Frankenstein inadvertently unleashed has been obliterated. The sacred channels of life run pure again, and Frankenstein's mysterious guilt has been atoned.

5

Poe and Initiation into the Sacred

In addition to the writers discussed thus far, many other eighteenth- and nineteenth-century authors incorporated elements of the numinous in their work. In an appendix to Rudolf Otto's *The Idea of the Holy,* Leonard Harvey suggests a number of examples, including passages from Wordsworth's *Prelude,* Coleridge's "Kubla Khan," and Blake's "Tiger! Tiger!"[1] Romantic writers seem particularly sensitive to this experience. On the other hand, one must not conclude that the Romantic and the numinous are identical. The most impassioned and lyrical outbursts—Keats's "Ode to a Nightingale," for example—may be entirely innocent of the numinous. In fact, intense "natural" emotions sometimes dissipate it, as in Hawthorne's *Scarlet Letter.*

Edgar Allan Poe, the writer whose work we examine next, represents the preeminent numinous literary figure of the early nineteenth century. It is perhaps for this reason that his work is a source of bewilderment if not downright annoyance to some critics. Poe's single-minded preoccupation with numinous themes tends to repel those of a critical-realist turn of mind, who see his work as lacking moral vitality and intellectual substance.[2] Some early exponents of this view were Emerson, who referred to him as "the jingle man," and Paul Elmore More, who characterized him as "the poet of boys and unripe men." This critical view of Poe is summed up in a well-known passage by T. S. Eliot: "That Poe has a powerful intellect, is undeniable; but it seems to me the intellect of a highly gifted young person before puberty. . . . There is just that lacking which gives dignity to a mature man: a consistent view of life."[3]

Such an opinion, of course, is not representative and in fact is hard to reconcile with Poe's high reputation in world literature, especially among the French.[4] According to Baudelaire, one of Poe's staunchest admirers,

> what will always make [Poe] worthy of praise is his preoccupation with all the truly important subjects and those which are alone worthy of the attention of a spiritual man: probabilities, mental illnesses, scientific hypotheses, hopes and considerations about a future life, analysis of the eccentrics and pariahs of this world, directly symbolic buffooneries. Add to this ceaseless and astonishing impartiality which is antithetical to his subjective nature, an extraordinary power of analysis and deduction, and the customary tautness of his writings—and it will not seem surprising that we have called him the *outstanding figure of his country*.[5]

Baudelaire's list of subjects "worthy of the attention of a spiritual man" clearly leans in the direction of Otto's nonrational. It is Poe's preoccupation with themes of alienation, the preternatural, and "the beyond" that elicits Baudelaire's praise. Baudelaire perceived what many of Poe's critics have missed: Poe was a mystic; beneath the sometimes flamboyant surface of his work lies a substantial body of visionary experience. Because Poe had no orthodox religious belief, the experience often takes eccentric form and direction;

close analysis, however, reveals a significant sense of unity. At its best, his work adumbrates the Western mystical tradition in many respects.[6] Once it is recognized, this numinous quality provides the consistency Eliot missed.

A good way to begin such an analysis is with a passage from a nonfiction work that Poe called *Marginalia*. In the quotation given below, we see Poe describing a kind of vision he apparently experienced at various times in his life. The passage is worth quoting in full, since it provides a basis from which the spiritual quality of his work may have arisen.

> There is, however, a class of fancies, of exquisite delicacy, which are *not* thoughts, and to which, as yet, I have found it absolutely impossible to adapt language. I use the word *fancies* at random and merely because I must use *some* word; but the idea commonly attached to the term is not even remotely applicable to the shadows of shadows in question. They seem to me rather psychal than intellectual. They arise in the soul (alas! how rarely!) only at epochs of the most intense tranquility—when the bodily and mental health are in perfection—and at those mere points in time where the confines of the waking world blend with those of the world of dreams. . . .
>
> These fancies have in them a pleasurable ecstasy as far beyond the most pleasurable of the world of wakefulness, or of dreams, as the Heaven of the Northman theology is beyond its Hell. I regard the visions, even as they arise, with an awe which, in some measure, moderates or tranquilizes the ecstasy—I so regard them through a conviction . . . that this ecstasy, in itself, is of a character supernal to the Human Nature—is a glimpse of the spirit's outer world. . . . It is as if the five senses were supplanted by five myriad others alien to mortality.[7]

Poe's experience places him in a tradition of nineteenth-century "nature mysticism" and is similar to accounts found in William James's *The Varieties of Religious Experience* and R. C. Zaehner's *Mysticism: Sacred and Profane.* One finds parallel visions in Emerson, Thoreau, Whitman, Wordsworth, and Tennyson, among others; but in Poe's case the perception seems especially close to that of Otto. Like the numinous, the experience is nonintellectual and difficult to express. The *fancies* Poe mentions arise at moments of tranquility; they are "awesome" and "supernal" and, like Otto's *mysterium tremendum et fascinans,* suggest an objective element in spiritual reality: "the spirit's outer world . . . as if the five senses were supplanted by five myriad others alien to mortality."

As depicted in this passage, the numinous emphasizes the moment of *fascinans:* ecstasy, tranquility, delight. Let us compare Poe's account with the following from Otto:

> I recall vividly a conversation I had with a Buddhist monk. He had been putting before me methodically and pertinaciously the arguments for the Buddhist "theology of negation," the doctrine of Anātman and "entire emptiness." When he had made an end, I asked him what then Nirvana itself is; and after a long pause came at last the single answer, low and restrained: "Bliss—unspeakable." And the hushed restraint of that answer, the solemnity of his voice, demeanour, and gesture made more clear what was meant than the words themselves.[8]

The numinous cuts across all religious lines and, paradoxically enough, can even be experienced by nonbelievers. A quotation from a nineteenth-century skeptic, Richard Jeffries, is instructive in this regard:

> I was utterly alone with the sun and the earth. Lying down on the grass, I spoke in my soul to the earth, the sun, the air, and the distant sea far beyond sight. . . . By all these, I prayed; I felt an emotion of the soul beyond all definition; prayer is a puny thing to it, and the word is a rude sign to the feeling, but I know no other. . . . Realizing the spirit,

recognizing my own inner consciousness, the psyche, so clearly, I cannot understand time. It is eternity now. I am in the midst of it. It is about me in the sunshine; I am in it, as the butterfly floats in the light laden air. Nothing has to come; it is now. Now is eternity; now is the immortal life. Here this moment, by this tumulus, on earth, now; I exist in it.[9]

Once it is recognized, the numinous element in Poe's work not only argues against the supposed inconsistency and lack of substance but obviates another charge: the narrowness of his critical theory of poetry. Poe's theoretical conjectures as to the origin and nature of the poetic impulse show a tacit recognition of the numinous, especially in its Dionysian or ecstatic movement, the *fascinans*. The poetic impulse springs from a faculty he calls *Ideality:* "The sense of the beautiful, the sublime, and the mystical." It has no necessary connection with "the passions of mankind" and excludes even "normal" human beauty: "He who would merely sing with whatever rapture . . . of the sights and sounds which greet him in common with all mankind . . . has yet failed to prove his divine title. . . . There is still a longing unsatisfied which he has been impotent to fulfill."[10]

The poet must base his work on a supernal, or numinous goal: "Inspired by an ecstatic prescience of the glories beyond the grave, we struggle by multiform combinations among the things and thoughts of Time, to attain a portion of the Loveliness whose very elements, perhaps, appertain to eternity alone."[11] In other words, Poe attempts to elevate the poetic to the numinous, a confusion no doubt but one bearing witness to the serious mystical impulse behind his work.

The numinous is most evident in Poe's prose tales. In these, admittedly, the numinous has been tacitly recognized, but at the cost of a misunderstanding. To most of his readers, Poe is conceded to be an artist of the terrifying and the gruesome. He is the concocter of sepulchral visions of vampirish ladies, premature burials, decaying mansions and cities, exquisitely sadistic tortures, and various sensational horrors.[12]

The sensational note (which no one denies) has been emphasized not only by the media but by certain critics who ought to know better; anyone who reads and rereads Poe's tales over a long period of time must recognize the one-sidedness of such a view. Admittedly a few of the major tales are merely frightening: "The Black Cat," "The Pit and the Pendulum," "The Tell-Tale Heart," "The Cask of Amontillado," "The Murders in the Rue Morgue." The list is short, however. Of the remaining major tales, one finds a characteristic blending of the fearful (the *mysterium tremendum*) with the supernally beautiful (the *fascinans*). The latter, more representative list would include "Manuscript Found in a Bottle," "A Descent into the Maelstrom," "Ligeia," "Morella," "Eleonora," "Berenice," "The Fall of the House of Usher," "The Island of the Fay," "William Wilson," "Metzengerstein," "The Assignation," "Shadow—A Parable," "Silence—A Fable"; and such mystical stories as "The Colloquy of Monos and Una," "The Conversation of Eiros and Charmion," and Poe's single novel, *The Narrative of Arthur Gordon Pym*.

In each of these tales, with varying emphasis, Poe's characteristic strategy is to lift the mind into a realm of spiritual reality in which the awesome, the alien, and the supernally beautiful combine in what Otto designated a "harmony of contrasts." To attain this goal Poe makes use of a pattern which, in one way or another, informs each tale. This pattern, which has epistemological overtones, is best described as initiation into the sacred. With only a few exceptions each story posits a narrator who is imbued with a "rational" outlook on life. As the story continues events of a "nonrational" character obtrude. These events, which may be either natural or preternatural, are of a daunting, even distressing nature and are best described by the anthropological and sociological term *rites of passage.* The pressure of such events culminates in a transformation of the narrator's view into the nonrational or *numinous*—the harmony of contrasts in which the daunting and the entrancing combine in a sacred epiphany.

This pattern clearly is evident in an early story, "The Manuscript Found in a Bottle."[13] The story opens with a characteristic statement by the narrator, a man of marked "rationalistic" views.

> Beyond all things, the study of the German moralists gave me great delight; not from any ill-advised admiration of their eloquent madness, but from the ease with which my habits of rigid thought enabled me to detect their falsities. I have often been reproached with the aridity of my genius; a deficiency of imagination has been imputed to me as a crime; and the Pyrrhonism of my opinions has at all times rendered me notorious. Indeed, a strong relish for physical philosophy has, I fear, tinctured my mind with a very common error of this age—I mean the habit of referring occurrences even the least susceptible of such reference, to the principles of that science. Upon the whole, no person could be less liable than myself to be led away from the severe precincts of truth by the *ignes fatui* of superstition.[14]

The irrational is, for the narrator, territory to be conquered, whether it appears as the "madness" of the German moralists [Kant, Schleiermacher?] or as mere superstition. A clear distinction is thus imposed between *rational* and *nonrational,* preparing the reader for the inevitable manifestation of the sacred.

Led on by "a kind of nervous restlessness which haunted me as a fiend," the narrator takes passage on a vessel bound from Batavia to the Archipelago of the Sunda Islands. A violent gale strikes the ship, killing all occupants except the narrator and an old Swedish sailor. Out of control, the ship is swept southward by strong winds, accompanied by mysterious phenomena that possess a quality of alien beauty. For example, the sun

> gave out no light, properly so called, but a dull and sullen glow without reflection, as if all its rays were polarized. Just before sinking within the turgid sea, its central fires suddenly went out, as if hurriedly extinguished by some unaccountable power. It was a dim, silver-like rim, alone, as it rushed down the unfathomable ocean.[15]

Such uncanny phenomena at last work their effect on the narrator's skepticism. "All around," he says, "were horror, and thick gloom, and a black sweltering desert of ebony. Superstitious terror crept by degrees into the spirit of the old Swede, and my own soul was wrapped up in silent wonder."[16]

The storm winds increase to hurricane force, and the ship now collides with an immense, leaden-hued vessel that bears down on it and upon which the narrator is hurled by the violence of the impact. The other vessel is manned by a crew of strange, sullen old men who neither speak nor take notice of the narrator. Their ancient Dutch costumes, the antiquity of the ship and its nautical equipment, and especially the unbroken silence combine to fill the narrator with a sense of fear, causing him to conceal himself. "An indefinite sense of awe, which at first sight of the navigators of the ship had taken hold of my mind, was perhaps the principle of my concealment. I was unwilling to trust myself with a race of people who had offered, to the cursory glance I had taken, so many points of vague novelty, doubt and apprehension."[17] As various preternatural incidents occur, however, this sense of awe becomes one of occult beauty.

The ship and all in it are imbued with the spirit of Eld.
The crew glide to and fro like the ghosts of buried centuries;
their eyes have an eager and uneasy meaning; and when
their fingers fall athwart my path in the wild glare of the
battle-lanterns, I feel as I have never felt before, although I
have been all my life a dealer in antiquities, and have im-
bibed the shadows of fallen columns at Balbec, and Tadmor
and Persepolis, until my very soul has become a ruin.[18]

As the ship nears the south polar region, the note of *fascinans* intensifies, dissipating the narrator's terror:

All in the immediate vicinity of the ship is the blackness of
eternal night, and a chaos of foamless water; but about a
league on either side of us, may be seen, indistinctly and at
intervals, stupendous ramparts of ice, towering away into
the desolate sky, and looking like the walls of the universe.
. . . To conceive the horror of my sensations is, I presume,
utterly impossible; yet a curiosity to penetrate the mysteries
of these awful regions, predominates even over my despair,
and will reconcile me to the most hideous aspect of death.
It is evident that we are hurrying onward to some exciting
knowledge—some never-to-be-imparted secret, whose at-
tainment is destruction.[19]

Having apparently reached the South Pole, the ship is
now hurled in "immense concentric circles, round and
round the borders of a gigantic amphitheatre, the summit
of whose walls is lost in the darkness and distance." Entering the confines of the whirlpool, the vessel is sucked down
but not, evidently, before the narrator has deposited his
manuscript in a bottle and tossed it overboard.

In this early prose narrative Poe describes with curious
exactness the various "notes" of numinous feeling, pro-
gressing from fear and awe, to wonder and at last to a kind
of fascination before the great mystery. There is a clear

alteration of the narrator's view from rational to nonrational, culminating in a sudden confrontation of the "harmony of contrasts" as the sacred mystery bursts upon him.[20]

The roots of the ontological conflict Poe dramatizes in this and other tales may be found in the period in which he lived. Like other nineteenth-century Romantics (notably Wordsworth), Poe was haunted by a sense of the loss of the sacred in the industrial society of his day. His tales can even be viewed as "protests" against what Mircea Eliade calls the "de-sacralizing tendencies" of modern society. There is a note of disorientation in his work which caused Allen Tate to speak of Poe as a "transitional figure in modern literature because he discovered our great subject, the disintegration of personality, but kept it in a language that had developed in a tradition of unity and order."[21]

This conflict, cosmological as well as sociological, takes on some peculiar forms in Poe's fiction. It can be seen with unmistakable clarity, however, in a tale Poe wrote later in his career and entitled "The Colloquy of Monos and Una." The story is a mystical account—half-literal, half-symbolic—of the passage of a soul from the present world to the beyond. The narrator of this angelic drama is a spirit named Monos, who dwells in Aidenn, the world beyond death. To Una, a newly arrived spirit in Aidenn, Monos recounts the transition of the soul from one form of being to the other. In the process he tells her in a brief précis what the world was like when he left it.

> Alas! we had fallen upon the most evil of all our evil days.
> The great "movement"—that was the cant term—went on:
> a diseased commotion, moral and physical. Art—the Arts—
> arose supreme, and, once enthroned, cast chains upon the
> intellect which had elevated them to power. Man, because
> he could not but acknowledge the majesty of Nature, fell
> into childish exultation at his acquired and still-increasing

dominion over her elements. Even while he stalked a God
in his own fancy, an infantine imbecility came over him. As
might be supposed from the origin of his disorder, he grew
infected with system, and with abstraction. He enwrapped
himself in generalities. . . . Man could not both know and
succumb. Meantime huge smoking cities arose, innumerable. Green leaves shrank before the hot breath of furnaces.
The fair face of Nature was deformed as with the ravages of
some loathsome disease. And methinks, sweet Una, even
our slumbering sense of the forced and the far-fetched might
have arrested us here. But it appears that we had worked
out our own destruction in the perversion of our *taste,* or
rather in the blind neglect of its culture in the schools. For,
in truth, it was at this crisis that taste alone—that faculty
which, holding a middle position between the pure intellect
and the moral sense, could never safely have been disre-
garded—it was now that taste alone could have led us gently
back to Beauty, to Nature, and to life. . . . But this thing was
not to be.[22]

Tate holds that this "flash of unsustained insight" has
"a greater dignity, a deeper philosophical perspective, and
a tougher intellectual fibre, than the academic exercises of
either Arnold or Mr. Richards."[23] The passage indeed reminds one of similar protests by Otto and Eliade against the
desacralizing processes of modern life. Poe sees modern
man as moving toward a condition in which the sheerly
rational and profane strip life of its mystery; in his vision,
man "stalked a God in his own fancy . . . grew infected with
system, and with abstraction," resulting in the profanation
of life itself: "The fair face of Nature was deformed as with
the ravages of some loathsome disease." And the faculty of
taste, by which man might have recovered, standing between the intellect and the moral sense, suggests analogi-
cally the *numinous* of Otto and the *sacred* of Eliade.[24]

The pattern throughout Poe's work suggests a kind of ontological search for the sacred. Lacking formal religious faith yet fully alive to the spiritual world, he sets forth in his poetry and especially in his fiction a process of initiation into the numinous. The result is a sort of archetypal pattern that he repeats over and over. Invariably the protagonists in these many-colored visions try to conceal, disguise, or, in a literal or figurative sense, bury the sacred impulses. This results in a conflict as the *mysterium* seeks to manifest itself. In some cases the character or characters undergo a series of ordeals—rites of passage in anthropological terms. In other cases the sacred entity simply bursts forth on its own, with the invariable result: the story ends with a profound confrontation of the numinous object.

The pattern varies slightly from tale to tale as Poe assigns a more or less active role to the protagonist. In some of the best stories, such as "Ligeia" or "The Fall of the House of Usher," the structure rests on a central narrator who is almost a passive observer and whose purpose seems to be that of convincing himself that what he sees is not real.[25] In other cases, such as "The Masque of the Red Death," the protagonist plays an active role in attempting to suppress or forestall the sacred epiphany. Also, it should be noted that the axiological qualities surrounding the numinous vary considerably. In such tales as "Morella," "Eleonora," and "The Island of the Fay," the numinous has an ecstatic quality. In a few, for example, "Ligeia," the *mysterium* seems "beyond good or evil." Even where the numinous is frightening or appalling, though, the note of weird and unearthly beauty is present. As we have noted, this quality lifts Poe's narrative range far beyond that of the merely terrifying.

For some reason, the mystic quality—as opposed to the merely frightening—frequently is evident in stories of the sea. We saw this in "The Manuscript Found in a Bottle," but an even better example is "A Descent into the Maelstrom," one of Poe's finest tales. The narrative begins with a vignette that acts as a symbolic motif for the action. The young, unnamed narrator of the tale and an old Norwegian fisherman have, after an arduous climb, reached the top of Mount Helseggen, a vast cliff on the western coast of Norway in the region of the Lofoten Islands. The old fisherman has brought the young man to this vantage point to show him the great Moskoeström—the Norwegian whirlpool—which at any instant now will become active. The old man also wishes to narrate, against this background, an amazing tale, "an event such as never happened before to mortal man— or at least such as no man has ever survived to tell of—and the six hours of deadly terror which I endured have broken me up body and soul." A note of mystery is added when the old fisherman says: "It took less than a single day to change these hairs from jetty black to white, to weaken my limbs, and to unstring my nerves."[26]

The ideogramic quality of this opening scene is evident when one recalls the crowded history of numinous events that have transpired on mountains. Eliade describes the "sacred mountain" of primitive legend as an *axis mundi* that connects heaven and earth and marks the highest point in the world.[27]

The young narrator now witnesses the Moskoeström, which suddenly becomes active. His description points up the contrasting qualities of terror and beauty:

> The ordinary accounts of this vortex had by no means pre-
> pared me for what I saw. That of Jonas Ramus, which is
> perhaps the most circumstantial of any, cannot impart the
> faintest concept either of the magnificence, or of the horror
> of the scene—or of the wild bewildering sense of *the novel*
> which confounds the beholder.[28]

At this point the narrative role shifts to the old Norwegian fisherman, who recounts his strange and thrilling tale. He explains how he and his two brothers were in the habit of taking their "schooner-rigged smack" among the islands and reefs that lie near the Moskoeström but always when it was quiet. On one such trip a hurricane struck them. Due to the delay, they found themselves driving straight into the storm. This is the beginning of the rites-of-passage theme which serves to lift the fisherman into an exalted sense of the sacred. In the following passage, the reader notes the way in which the feeling of terror is modulated by the note of supernal beauty that creeps in.

> By this time the first fury of the tempest had spent itself. . . .
> The seas which at first had been kept down by the wind,
> and lay flat and frothing, now got up into absolute moun-
> tains. A singular change, too, had come over the heavens.
> Around in every direction it was still as black as pitch, but
> nearly overhead there burst out, all at once, a circular rift of
> clear sky—as clear as I ever saw—and bright blue—and
> through it there blazed forth the full moon with a lustre that
> I never before knew her to wear. She lit up everything about
> us with the greatest distinctness—but Oh God, what a scene
> it was to light up.[29]

The note of *fascinans,* symbolized by the blue sky and bright moon, continues to evolve like a mysterious counter-point. As the rites of passage proceed, the fearsome and daunting emotions lessen and the *fascinans* emerges:

> It may look like boasting—but what I tell you is the truth—
> I began to reflect how magnificent a thing it was to die in
> such a manner, and how foolish it was in me to think of so
> paltry a consideration as my own individual life, in view of
> the wonderful manifestation of God's power. . . . I positively
> felt a *wish* to explore its depths, even at the sacrifice I was

going to make; and my principal grief was that I should never be able to tell my old companions on shore about the mysteries I should see.[30]

The fisherman's smack now enters the heart of the Moskoeström as the story reaches its emotional climax:

> Never shall I forget the sensations of awe, horror, and admiration with which I gazed about me. The boat appeared to be hanging, as if by magic, midway down, upon the interior surface of a funnel vast in circumference, prodigious in depth, and whose perfectly smooth sides might have been mistaken for ebony, but for the bewildering rapidity with which they spun around, and for the gleaming and ghastly radiance they shot forth, as the rays of the full moon, from that circular rift amid the clouds which I have already described, streamed in a flood of golden glory along the black walls, and far away down into the inmost recesses of the abyss.[31]

It would be difficult to find a single passage in Gothic literature that encapsulates the numinous more fully. Poe's explicit reference to "awe, horror, and admiration" (the harmony of contrasts) leads to the nearly preternatural image of the little boat, hanging "as if by magic" amid the whirl. The feeling of sublimity is then aroused by the description of the ebony waters swirled about at immense velocity, a feeling that is modulated into a growing sense of *fascinans* as the moon streams "in a flood of golden glory" down the black walls and into the abyss (the *mysterium*).

At this point in the tale the fisherman has undergone a series of rites of passage and has reached the final stage, or level, of the soul's journey into the sacred.[32] Poe reinforces this feeling by an image drawn from anthropology. The reference in the following passage to the mysterious Bridge of the Mussulmen is strikingly modern in its context:

The rays of the moon seemed to search the very bottom of the profound gulf; but still I could make out nothing distinctly, on account of the thick mist in which everything here was enveloped, and over which there hung a magnificent rainbow, like that narrow and tottering bridge which Mussulmen say is the only pathway between Time and Eternity. This mist, or spray, was no doubt occasioned by the clashing of the great walls of the funnel, as they all met together at the bottom—but the yell that went up to the Heavens from out of that mist, I dare not attempt to describe.[33]

A comment by Mircea Eliade suggests the legendary quality of this rites-of-passage image:

But it is especially the images of the *bridge* and the *narrow gate* which suggest the idea of a dangerous passage and which, for this reason, frequently occur in initiatory and funerary rituals and mythologies. Initiation, death, mystical ecstasy, absolute knowledge, "faith" in Judeo Christianity—all these are equivalent to passage from one mode of being to another and bring about a veritable ontological mutation. To suggest this paradoxical passage (for it always implies a break and a transcendence) the various religious traditions have made plentiful use of the symbolism of the Perilous Bridge and the Narrow Gate.[34]

The story has moved to its numinous climax. It now returns to the realm of the rational as the old fisherman details the means of his escape from the maelstrom and his subsequent rescue by comrades. His comrades, however, scarcely recognize him. A change has occurred: "They knew me no more than they would have known a traveller from the spirit-land. My hair, which had been raven-black the day before, was as white as you see it now. They say too that the whole expression had changed." The fisherman, in going through the rites of passage and confronting the *sacer* of the numinous, has moved into a different ontological plane from his comrades. He has in a sense passed from the profane to the sacred. But the profound insight he has gained is not available to anyone else. "I told them my story—they did not believe it. I now tell it to you—and I can scarcely expect you to put more faith in it than did the merry fishermen of Lofoten."[35]

6

The Numinous Aesthetic of Henry James

At first glance, Henry James might seem an unlikely candidate for a place among numinous writers. The major portion of his fiction is solidly realistic and though refined and subtle lacks all connection with the supernatural. The background of his stories, albeit limited to an aristocratic milieu, is rendered with great accuracy. Similarly, the motivation of his characters is perfectly convincing in terms of normal human psychology.

Despite this massive achievement, James is today recognized as one of the masters of the ghostly tale. In a half-dozen stories and in one short novel, he created a distinct body of supernatural literature that stands unrivaled for depth and artistic power. More than this, his influence on the development of the ghost story was profound, for he created an aesthetic for the numinous story: a set of working principles by means of which such tales achieve artistic perfection.

It would seem that supernatural literature would by rights have held little appeal to James. He himself admitted that he wanted to study life by reflecting on human consciousness. His criterion for a story was the amount of "felt life" it contained. Nothing could have been more inimical to him than the creation of mere "effect." Elements of plot, setting, and characterization in his work exist for the sake of the "finely wrought consciousness" or "point of view" James sought to elicit. One might imagine that a mere ghost would be too crude an object for him. Among other problems, how would he fit it into the social scale?

Paradoxically, it was James's interest in consciousness and the subtleties of human imagination that brought him into contact with numinous literature. Although he was not a believer in the supernatural in the ordinary meaning of the word, his ghostly tales hint at a strong underlying fascination with the sort of ontological questions with which we have been dealing. In the ghost story, as in other forms of fiction, the question of belief, or "felt life," is uppermost. A glance at the vast critical literature that has emerged over the question of the real or fancied existence of the ghosts at Bly in *The Turn of the Screw* proves this. Everyone who has read it feels—and rightly so—that the epistemological question must be resolved in order for the story to be fully appreciated. James's answer, as I attempt to show, was to merge the epistemological with the aesthetic question. The ghosts "exist" but in the larger context of artistic exploration. This numinous aesthetic springs from the same a priori source that Otto investigated; the numinous is objective—a sense of "presence"—yet it is known primarily through the feelings.

James's interest in the occult may have come to him by way of his father. The senior Henry was an avowed disciple of the mystical doctrines of Emanuel Swedenborg and spent most of his life studying metaphysics and theology, especially their more esoteric aspects. As a young man, and while recuperating from the loss of a leg, he had experienced what he was later to call a "vastation." The vastation was a frightening apparition of a demon standing beside the fireplace of his New York apartment. A mental breakdown of some sort followed this uncanny vision, and he sought doctor after doctor, to no avail. Henry James, Sr. apparently was cured of the effects of this trauma by a study of the mystical doctrines of Swedenborg. This strange experience, not unknown in the history of psychic research, established his lifelong interest in mysticism and the occult.[1]

Henry James's brother, William, was also a student of psychic phenomena. Not only did he help found the American branch of the Society for Psychical Research, William was a lifelong student of telepathy and other activities which today are called extrasensory perception.[2]

Henry James wrote his first ghost story, "The Romance of Certain Old Clothes," in 1868 and continued to write occasionally in this genre throughout his career. Altogether, there are ten stories that can be considered true ghostly tales, and several others hint at the supernatural. Leon Edel, who has edited these stories, says that James "wrote two kinds of ghost stories: those in which ghosts appear and do their haunting, and those in which no ghosts show themselves. But we see in both the inner-haunted individual in all his uneasiness and anxiety."[3]

This inner-haunted individual is, in all the ghost stories of James, the focal point at which his obsession with point of view merges with and expands into his feeling for the numinous. The method is evident in one of his early tales, "The Ghostly Rental" (1875). This story is especially interesting in that, while the events are all perfectly natural, the story projects a strong sense of the uncanny, indicating that James possessed some theoretical understanding of the numinous at an early point in his career.

The story is narrated by a young student at Harvard Divinity School. In the opening section James makes it clear that this young man is a thoroughgoing "rationalist," of the sort Poe often used, as we saw in Chapter 5. The young narrator is an admirer of William Ellery Channing (a nineteenth-century theologian who attempted to strip Christianity of dogmatism and wed it to reason). He favors such a theology because he feels it offers "the rose of faith delightfully stripped of its thorns," and he favored the Harvard Divinity School as the "tranquil home of mild casuistry."[4]

Walking alone in the environs of the college one day, the narrator chances upon an ancient, sinister-looking house that lies at the end of a deserted road. It is twilight, and the house, bathed in a crepuscular glow, exudes an aura of the occult. "The house is simply haunted," the student mutters. "Half an hour before, if I had been asked, I would have said, as befitted a young man who was explicitly cultivating cheerful views of the supernatural, that there were no such things as haunted houses. But the dwelling before me gave a vivid meaning to the empty words; it had been spiritually blighted."[5]

Fascinated by the mysterious atmosphere of the house, the young man visits it a second time and on this occasion observes an elderly man covertly leaving it. After making some inquiries, the student meets the old man and learns his story. He is Captain Diamond, a retired soldier, and he relates the circumstances of his mysterious visits to the abandoned house. Many years earlier he and his daughter had quarreled over a suitor of hers whom the father distrusted. As a result, the old man banished his daughter. Afterward, she presumably died, but her spirit took possession of the house. As it turns out, the daughter "rents" the house from her credulous old father, who visits it once every three months to receive his "ghostly rental."

Intrigued by Captain Diamond's story, the student befriends him and in due time asks to accompany him on one of his quarterly visits to collect the rent. The student's hopes for a confrontation with the spirit are amply fulfilled. The description of this ghostly encounter, with its careful delineation of the various feeling-states of the numinous, clearly demonstrates that James was thinking along lines similar to those of Otto:

> Suddenly, with an inexpressible sensation, I became aware that this gloom was animated; it seemed to move and gather itself together. Slowly—I say slowly, for to my tense expectancy the instants appeared ages—it took the shape of a large, definite figure, and this figure advanced and stood at the top of the stairs. I frankly confess that by this time I was conscious of a feeling to which I am in duty bound to apply the vulgar name of fear. I may poeticize it and call it Dread, with a capital letter.[6]

The numinous implications of this scene, with its suggested distinction between "fear" and "Dread," mark the tale as an early and perhaps immature attempt by Henry James to explore the ontological and aesthetic regions he depicted in later ghostly tales. Indeed, the young narrator of this story attempts to impose an epistemological solution on the matter by taking what he calls a "sternly rational view." In a later analysis of the event, however, he struggles to differentiate between rational and nonrational, between the numinous and the merely natural:

> Certainly I had seen *something*—that was not fancy; but what had I seen? I regretted extremely now that I had not been bolder, that I had not gone nearer and inspected the apparition more minutely. . . . Was not this paralyzation of my powers in itself a supernatural influence? Not necessarily, perhaps, for a sham ghost that one accepted might do

perhaps as much execution as a real ghost. But why had I
so easily accepted the sable phantom that waved its hand?
Why had it so impressed itself? . . . I greatly preferred that
it should have been true. . . . I tried, therefore, to let my
vision rest and to stop turning it over. But an impulse
stronger than my will recurred at intervals and set a mocking
question on my lips.[7]

The mocking question the narrator is concerned with—
the reality of the numinous apparition—is one James returned to in his later tales. At this point it is answered in
what, from an artistic standpoint, one may consider an
unsatisfactory manner, along the rational lines employed
earlier by Ann Radcliffe: the student narrator learns that
Captain Diamond is dying. Sent by the old man to make
the regular quarterly "collection," the young student confronts the spirit, unmasks it, and learns, as one might guess,
that it is Captain Diamond's daughter, still very much alive.
Out of a pettish desire to revenge herself on her father for
spurning her, she has carried out the elaborate hoax through
the years and duped the credulous old man. She is, of
course, duly repentant. Not satisfied with the somewhat
anticlimactic resolution, James adds what some might consider a trick ending. In a later meeting with the daughter the
student learns that she is now regularly visited by the apparition of her father, who apparently will haunt her as she
has haunted him. The ending muddies the distinction between real and unreal, rational and nonrational. The young
author cannot decide between a literal ghost and a projection
of the numinous impulse; the story does indicate, however,
that James was aware of the ontological implications of
stories in this genre and throws much light on the subsequent development of his writing.

"The Ghostly Rental" suggests that from the beginning
of his career James possessed an innate understanding of

the numinous. In the passage just quoted, the narrator makes a distinction between fear and dread—a distinction Otto often stressed. Later, after the narrator has rationalized the experience and "seen through it," he remains aware of its psychic influences.[8] At the story's end, James seems to suggest that a larger reality may lie behind the experience, as Captain Diamond's daughter succumbs to the occult feelings she previously invoked in her father and becomes a prey to the "haunting" she has instigated.

The story reveals as well James's awareness that the ghostly element must be grounded in a realistic, or "rational," context. Psychological realism was James's strong point; in his ghost stories he brought the weight of his powers to bear in such a way as to surround the nonrational core with a fully developed rational framework. He is, I believe, the first major supernatural writer to realize the absolute importance of surface realism in the production of Coleridge's "willing suspension of disbelief." Certainly Ann Radcliffe, Matthew Gregory Lewis, Mary Shelley, and to some extent Edgar Allan Poe had worked in this direction, but it was left to James to bring the process to perfection. Since his time no writer of the supernatural has successfully neglected this essential ingredient.

It is important to note that the realism is not, for James, "scientific realism." By the time he came to write the masterful *Turn of the Screw* in 1898, he had worked out the implications of "The Ghostly Rental" and had come to realize that the realism required for supernatural fiction differed from that of ordinary literature. In the well-known preface to *The Turn of the Screw,* he speaks condescendingly of the kind of ghostly tale in which matters are set forth on a "scientific" basis:

The new type indeed, the mere modern "psychical" case, washed clean of all queerness as by exposure to a flowing laboratory tap, and equipped with credentials vouching for this—the new type clearly promised little, for the more it was respectably certified, the less it seemed of a nature to rouse the dear old sacred terror.[9]

By this "new type" of ghost story James refers to the investigations of the recently founded Society for Psychical Research, led by Myers, Crookes, Barrett, and others, including James's own brother, William. James was saying that the attempt to "rationalize" the ghost story robs it of its essence. The "dear old sacred terror" (his apt synonym for the numinous) recedes before the spirit of mere logic and science. The *mysterium* must remain; otherwise, the central experience is crowded out and vanishes. As James put it, such tales depend on "a 'tone,' the tone of suspected and felt trouble, of an inordinate and incalculable sort—the tone of tragic, yet of exquisite, mystification."[10]

This "mystification," however, does not consist of the mere piling up of wonders; it must be a sort of fairy tale, yet one "springing from an artless and measureless, but from a conscious and cultivated credulity." In a word, it must have "roundness"—a feeling of balance. Mere elaborate flights of fancy (James mentions the *Arabian Nights*) are insufficient.[11]

The roundness required in such matters demands of the writer a rigid economy. Certain elements (for example, characterization), which might more strongly be emphasized in ordinary fiction, must be rigidly pruned in the ghost story. Concerning *The Turn of the Screw,* some critics have charged that James did not develop sufficiently the character of the governess. He was criticized for not endowing her "with signs and marks and features and humours, [he] hadn't, in a word, invited her to deal with her own mystery as well as that of Peter Quint, Miss Jessell, and the hapless children." To such criticism, James replied: "We have surely as much of her own nature as we can swallow in watching it reflect her anxieties and inductions.''[12] The governess has ''authority,'' and that is enough; anything more would be a distraction from the major point of the tale: the overall tone of mystification, of the numinous.

Here we come to a point already touched on. The supernatural tale requires a strategy different from that of ordinary fiction. Because the numinous must emerge on its own, so to speak, the author of a ghost story must, before all else, cultivate the proper sense of balance—James calls it ''roundness.'' Any strong or deliberate effect, whether of characterization or plot, can throw the mechanism out of gear. Elements that might be advantageous in other kinds of fiction can in the supernatural tale become liabilities. This explains James's aversion to scientific accounts of ghostly visitations, such as those recorded by the Society of Psychical Research. ''Recorded and attested ghosts,'' he said, ''are . . . as little expressive, as little dramatic, above all as little continuous and conscious and responsive, as is consistent with their taking the trouble . . . to appear at all.''[13] The ghosts attested to by science are not artistic ghosts; they may convince the reason, but they do nothing for the feelings and hence cannot arouse the sense of *mysterium*. Ghostly tales (James called them *amusettes*) may be the result of ''cold artistic calculation,'' but the calculation must be hidden from the reader in order for such works to breathe their unearthly atmosphere.

In *The Turn of the Screw* such artistic calculation forced on James the choice of

having my apparitions correct or having my story ''good''— that is, producing my impression of the dreadful, my designed horror. Good ghosts, speaking by book, make poor subjects, and it was clear from the first my hovering, prowling, blighting presences, my pair of abnormal agents, would have to depart altogether from the rules. They would be agents in fact; there would be laid on them the dire duty of causing the situation to reek with the air of Evil.[14]

The "air of Evil"—the sense of dread—lies at the heart of what Otto called the "negative numinous," a curious offshoot of the sacred. The author must seize on a subject that *suggests* this horrific note without specifying it exactly. A razor's edge must be walked between the demands of realism and the dangers of a pedestrian verisimilitude which would turn the uncanny into the scientific. James's aesthetic principle reminds one of Otto's warning against rationalizing the numinous in religion.

The subject of *The Turn of the Screw*—the *donnée,* in Jamesian language—came to its author in a setting that heightened its effect on him. On a cold winter day in 1895, and with the failure of his play *Guy Domville* still on his mind, James had traveled from London to Canterbury to visit an old friend, Archbishop Edward Benson White, at his estate at Addington Park. There, gathered around a hall-fire in the afternoon, "the talk turned, on I forget what homely pretext, to apparitions and nightfears, to the marked and sad drop in the general supply and still more in the general quality of such commodities." Amid the general lament for "the beautiful lost form," the archbishop himself recollected one such tale.

The impression made on him as a young man by the with-held glimpse, as it were, of a dreadful matter that had been reported years before, and with as few particulars, to a lady with whom he had youthfully talked. The story would have been thrilling could she but have found herself in better possession of it, dealing as it did with a couple of small children in an out-of-the-way place, to whom the spirits of certain "bad" servants, dead in the employ of the house,

were believed to have appeared with the design of "getting
hold" of them. . . . I was to remember the haunted children
and the prowling servile spirits as a "value" of the disquiet-
ing sort, in all conscience sufficient.[15]

This "precious pinch"—which James wrote up in his
notebook when he returned to London—continued to exert
its fascination. In his note James adds: "It is all obscure
and imperfect, the picture, the story, but there is a suggestion
of strangely gruesome effect in it. The story to be told—
tolerably obviously—by an outside spectator, observer."[16]
Thus the two central elements of such tales, the rational and
the nonrational, opened up before James; but it was the
latter that fascinated him. It was the "withheld glimpse" or
"shadow of a shadow" that determined his artistic purpose.

In reconstructing this purpose one must first clear the way
through a veritable jungle of commentary and criticism that
has grown up around the story. Few works as short as *The
Turn of the Screw* have elicited as much critical interpretation. The problem with this critical material is that, while
it is useful in explaining the intellectual content of the tale,
it tends to distract the reader from the central, or numinous,
goal—in James's words, "to scare the whole world." In
fact, one must take seriously, I think, James's later dis-
claimer to a woman who told him she did not understand
the meaning of the story: "no more do I . . . it just gleams
and glooms."[17]

In conceding the nonrational, or numinous, purpose of
the story James was careful in remarks made later to explain
the manner in which this occult element was arranged or
embedded in a rational (or realistic) setting. If, as in the
older Gothic literature, ghosts are merely frightening ("good
ghosts," in James's phrase), the air of mystery is lost; any
extreme definitiveness can dissipate the intended vision. It
is undoubtedly for this reason that James chose as his

narrator a sensible governess with a well-regulated mind. "I had about my young woman to take a very sharp line," he confessed in a letter to H. G. Wells. "The grotesque business I had to make her picture and the childish psychology I had to make her trace and present, were, for me at least, a very difficult job, in which absolute lucidity and logic . . . were imperative. Therefore, I had to rule out subjective complications of her own."[18]

To intensify this rational element, James was driven to the use of the multiple-frame story in which several narrative layers stand between the reader and the central events at Bly. First comes the unnamed narrator, who serves as a kind of neutral screen or tabula rasa. He and the other guests have gathered at a private party in an unidentified manor house in England, where they engage in telling ghost stories. One of the tales, concerning a small boy and his mother who are visited by a frightful apparition, is described by the narrator as "gruesome." Next we have a brief narration by Douglas, the host, who hints that he knows a similar story which he might relate. Questioned about the tale, he describes it as "Beyond everything. Nothing at all I know touches it." The quality it exudes is one of "dreadfulness!" After this, Douglas describes the circumstances by means of which he learned the story, and in his account we learn certain incidental details about the governess. She is twenty years old, the youngest daughter of a poor country parson, and from all indications a very reliable person. These successive layers, or frames, along with the businesslike account of the hiring of the governess, create an impression of the ordinary while, at the same time, insinuating a mysterious element lurking in the background.[19] In this, as in all numinous literature, the *mysterium* gathers itself about the routine, pedestrian aspects of reality. In no other form of writing does one find a greater reliance on convention and decorum.

Thus by the time we reach the central narrative—the governess's manuscript—we have been cleverly prepared to accept both its verisimilitude (the rational) and some incongruities, some "dreadfulness" (the nonrational). It is at this point that James moves to dissipate the rational, to make way for the nonrational.

Background, or ambience, is important in all numinous literature, so important that in some of the best stories it appears at times to crowd out other elements. There are superb ghost stories in which the setting becomes, in effect, the chief character. As we have seen, the means by which the numinous background is created are discussed by Otto in *The Idea of the Holy;* central to his concept are negative qualities, namely, darkness, silence, and empty space, all of which are subsumed under the term *isolation.* Such qualities predominate in the descriptive passages of *The Turn of the Screw.* The loneliness and isolation of the great house at Bly—its crenelated towers, winding passages, turrets, and vacant spaces—surround the reader with an aura of magic and enchantment.[20] Observing the vastness of the structure "in the presence of which I found myself," the governess admits that she is "freshly, a little scared not less than a little proud."[21] A feeling of loneliness pervades the neighborhood as though house and grounds were enchanted. "Everything at Bly is silent," Virginia Woolf once commented on the story.[22] Even Mrs. Grose, the rather mundane housekeeper, feels it and is glad beyond measure when the governess arrives. All these negative qualities are modulated into an aura of the uncanny, a sense of something "not quite right" at Bly. In the mind of the governess it takes the form of disorientation and a hint of spiritual blight.

> Wasn't it just a story-book over which I had fallen a-doze and a-dream? No, it was a big ugly antique but convenient house, embodying a few features of a building still older,

half displaced and half utilized, in which I had the fancy of
our being almost as lost as a handful of passengers in a great
drifting ship. Well, I was strangely at the helm![23]

Having established the rational and nonrational distinctions in the frame of the story and in its setting, James's
next task is to project this dichotomy in the characters. The
cast of the tale is limited, select. The nonrational, or fairy-
like, quality of the children Miles and Flora is deliberately
contrasted with the unimaginative character of Mrs. Grose.
Like the governess, she is reasonable and prudent, a model
of the British hierarchy of social values. With no hint of
servility she is "respectable," and she knows her place. She
and the governess form a rational background for the hints
of mystery the children cast over the story. When Miles is
inexplicably dismissed from the private school he attends,
both Mrs. Grose and the governess react with blank wonder.
Their discussion of the matter leads, by innuendo, to an
account of the previous governess, Miss Jessel. Hints of
some strange muted corruption fall like shadows, without
clear definition. These hints, or inklings, accumulate, reach-
ing a climax early in the story in the famous scene where
the governess spies the apparition of Peter Quint standing
at dusk on the crenelated tower of the house. As the scene
occurs, the governess does not perceive it as a "magical
event"; but its *effect* is clearly in this direction:

> The place moreover, in the strangest way in the world, had
> on the instant and by the very fact of its appearance become
> a solitude. . . . It was as if, while I took in, what I did take
> in, all the rest of the scene had been stricken with death. I
> can hear again, as I write, the intense hush in which the
> sounds of evening dropped. The rooks stopped cawing in
> the golden sky and the friendly hour lost for the unspeakable
> minute all its voice. . . . We were confronted across our

distance quite long enough for me to ask myself with intensity who then he was and to feel, as an effect of my inability to say, a wonder that in a few seconds became intense.[24]

It is interesting to compare the manner in which James modulates the various numinous moments in the scene with the ideas of Rudolf Otto. The place becomes "a solitude"; it is as though it were "stricken with death"; the "sounds of evening dropped"; the rooks cease their cawing; and the two figures, facing each other across the distance, produce a "wonder that . . . became intense."

The "blighted presence" of Peter Quint and of Miss Jessel are discussed by James in the preface to the story, which came later. They are not, he says, "ghosts" at all but are more akin to goblins, elves, imps, or demons. In the preface James compares them with the shadowy, spectral figures "in the old trials of witchcraft." It was necessary that the reader should feel their sinister quality without having it formalized. How, he asks, could he otherwise establish the menacing note without "the drop, the comparative vulgarity, inevitably attending . . . the offered example, the imputed vice, the cited act, the limited deplorable presentable instance?"[25]

This sense of unspecified evil takes us back to Otto's conception of profanity, discussed in Chapter 4, *Frankenstein.* "The feeling," Otto says, "is beyond question not that of the transgression of the moral law, however evident it may be that such a transgression, where it has occurred, will involve it as a consequence; it is the feeling of absolute profaneness." Succeeding glimpses of the two servants accentuate this feeling. Quint is, by turns, a "horror," "no gentleman," a "hound," a "detestable living presence." Miss Jessel is an "alien object," "dreadful," an "unmistakable horror and evil." Despite these qualifications, there are only a few hints of actual, concrete wrongdoing.[26] James suggests sexual adventurism on the part of Quint; he "had his way" with the other servant girls, and it is evident that he had corrupted Miss Jessel. Similarly, the pair had in some obscure way "taught" the children bad ways, but the teaching is left shadowy, deliberately so. The point to note is that James, in tacit agreement with Otto, suggests an indeterminate sense of "lostness" on the part of the two servants.

Of this concept, Otto says:

> In this sense, therefore, "lostness" is something which both in its first and in its deepest sense had nothing whatever to do with psychological considerations regarding the directive influence of lower or higher motives upon our will or with the problem of moral freedom of the will and its range of moralistic action. Lostness is the natural profanity lying outside of moral values and not to be overcome by an act of volition; it is the incapacity to find or to appreciate the divine object, before or without its own revelation.[27]

This fugitive feeling is subtly focused in the several appearances of Miss Jessel. She projects a sense of despair that borders on sorrow or melancholy. "Looking down it from the top I once recognized the presence of a woman seated on one of the lower steps with her back presented to me, her body half-bowed and her head, in an attitude of woe, in her hands."[28] Later:

> She rose, not as if she had heard me, but with an indescribable grand melancholy of indifference and detachment, and, within a dozen feet of me, stood there as my vile predecessor. Dishonored and tragic she was all before me. . . . Dark as midnight in her black dress, her haggard beauty and her unutterable woe.[29]

The sense of lostness is spelled out directly when the governess apprises Mrs. Grose of what she has seen:

"I found her, on my return, in the school room."

"And what did she say?" I can hear the good woman still and the candour of her stupefaction. "That she suffers the torments—!"

It was this, of a truth, that made her, as she filled out my picture, gape. "Do you mean," she faltered, "—of the lost?"

"Of the lost. Of the damned. And that's why, to share them—?"

"She wants Flora."[30]

Such hints and suggestions call to mind a far stronger sense of the reality of evil than would an itemized list of particular sins. This same deliberate lack of definition extends to the mode of existence of Quint and Miss Jessel. Thus James chose to project them as visions of spiritual reality rather than as what he called "good ghosts."

This artistically correct choice has left the story open to a variety of misinterpretations, however. Some critics— among them, Edmund Wilson—allowed themselves to be misled by the question of whether the apparitions of the servants are "real." Concluding (as Wilson did) that they are not real, Wilson, in his well-known essay, sought to discover the psychological mechanism by means of which the governess projects them. "The theory," he said, "is, then, that the governess who is made to tell the story is a neurotic case of sex repression, and that the ghosts are not real ghosts but hallucinations of the governess.[31] The evidence that Wilson adduced for this theory is brief and tenuous. It consists mainly of pointing out that, as far as the reader is told, no one other than the governess actually sees the ghosts of Quint and Miss Jessel. It is on this slight foundation that Wilson argued his thesis.

Wilson's essay has been answered a number of times, by some excellent critics, who have tried to show that his Freudian interpretation of the story is based solely on conjecture and that it lacks genuine factual evidence.[32] It would be tedious, and perhaps useless, to rehearse these arguments. The clearest argument against Wilson's thesis, it seems to me, is that this viewpoint deprives *Turn of the Screw* of the numinous element James labored so diligently to create. If Quint's and Miss Jessel's apparitions are not "real"—at least in some sense of the word—the *mysterium* vanishes and with it the entire point of James's comments in his preface to the story. The question should not be, Are the ghosts real? but, rather, What is the *mode* of their existence? This question is best answered by relying on Otto's theories.

James's purpose, as I have attempted to prove in this chapter, was to project his vision of the numinous in the most artistically sound arrangement of structure that he could provide. Setting, character, and story are joined in an exquisite balance that directs and orders the mind and feelings to a vision of the nonrational. James once remarked in jest, "the story gleams and glooms"—but it is a jest that conceals a world of meaning.

7

The Daemonic in *Dracula*

Bram Stoker's *Dracula* is one of those rare novels that merits the timeworn phrase "it needs no introduction." Since its publication in 1897 the book has established an undeniable claim on the public imagination. Not only has it passed through innumerable editions (including foreign translations), it has entered the domain of popular culture through constant dramatizations, including radio, motion pictures, and television. The world has taken the book's grim protagonist to its heart in a way reserved for only a few mythical figures. In another decade *Dracula* will celebrate its hundredth anniversary, the benchmark Samuel Johnson thought should be the required testing period for a classic.

As with certain other works of supernatural literature, however, public approbation has done little to enhance the book's critical reputation. For reasons already set forth, supernatural literature has fared poorly among scholars and critics; consequently popular approval may at times prove to be a liability. It is only in recent years, with the rise of a more eclectic spirit in scholarly studies, that the novel has received any comment at all.[1] It should be clear, however, that the novel, like its vampire protagonist, is not going to die an easy death. Critics who in the past have not bothered to taste its strange contents (to continue the spectral metaphor) might well consider doing so. Far too much attention has been paid to *Dracula*'s supposed weaknesses and not enough to its central strengths.[2]

The alleged weaknesses turn out to be of the same type that critics assign to the entire genre of supernatural tales: lack of relationship to the major themes of realistic literature. Critics who take such a view (for example, Edmund Wilson) cannot respond to the strengths of Gothic literature without attempting to rationalize the supernatural element in it. Impervious to the numinous core of this genre, they continually attempt to turn it into something else—repressed sexuality, sociology, Marxism, or whatever is at hand. An extreme example of this tendency is seen in Glen St. John Barclay's discussion of *Dracula* in his delightful but wrongheaded study, *Anatomy of Horror*. Despite the humor that informs Barclay's work, Barclay manages thoroughly to misconceive the nature of many of the books he discusses, including *Dracula*. Stoker, he says, "has in the first place the deficiency commonly found among writers who concern themselves almost exclusively with occult themes of having either no interest in human personality, or no ability to analyze it."[3] This, as explained above, is to mistake the purpose of such literature; it is like complaining that a limerick is not sufficiently metaphysical or that *Oedipus Rex* is not duly concerned with political theory.

A myopic view such as this leads Barclay into all sorts of misinterpretations. Jonathan Harker is simply "half-witted." The several women in the story "acquire the faintest interest as human beings only when they begin to turn into vampires." Finally, Barclay is led to the logical impasse of attempting to explain the book's undeniable popularity as the result of repressed sexuality: "towering erotic symbolism, which is what *Dracula* is all about." The vampires, Barclay assures us, are "incarnations of sexual desire"; the passages in which they pursue their bloodletting are "the literary equivalent of orgasm." The scene in which Lucy is impaled by Van Helsing and her suitors is an example of mutual rape culminating in mutual orgasm. And so on. It never seems to occur to Barclay (whose pungent wit deserts him) that if such a reading is correct—if the appeal lies in sublimated sexuality—the book would of necessity have died a natural death in an age like ours when explicit sexual description is all too common. Despite his keen humor (for example, the proper background music for the impalement of Lucy would be the "Anvil Chorus"), Barclay's conclusions are ultimately of the sort Edmund Wilson arrived at in his reading of James's *The Turn of the Screw*.

Fortunately more substantial assessments of the book are available. For example, David Punter recognizes that *Dracula* "is not only a well-written and formally investive novel but also one of the most important expressions of social and psychological dilemmas of the late nineteenth century." Sensing a mythic quality in the book, he sees it in essence as "the inversion of Christianity and particularly of Pauline Christianity in that Dracula promises and gives—the real resurrection of the body, but disunited from the soul."[4]

The suggestion of Christian symbolism is echoed by Leonard Wolf. According to Wolf, Dracula takes on the aspect of an anti-Christ as he seeks to spread his infection to others. Wolf points out a number of biblical and Christian references, including vampire-like sacraments of baptism and marriage.[5]

Both Punter and Wolf approach the book in what I believe is the correct way, for *Dracula* more clearly than other Gothic works of fiction dramatizes the cosmic struggle between the opposing forces of darkness and light, of the sacred and the profane. Indeed, this antinomy which we have seen in other works of the occult is at the heart of *Dracula,* where it takes on the proportions of a worldwide struggle, sweeping racial, geographical, even ontological counters in its wake. The actors in the story, whether human or superhuman, take on symbolic significance, so that they become surrogates for traditions, cultural forces, and races of people of Europe and Asia.

These ideogramic structures are glimpsed in the novel's dramatic opening section. The story begins with a seemingly prosaic account from a journal kept by Jonathan Harker, a London solicitor. At the request of the law firm for which he works, Harker undertakes a journey across Europe to the Carpathian Mountains. There, in a castle set among the mountains, he is to meet with a client of the firm, a certain Count Dracula, and work out business arrangements for the Count's intended move to England. Harker reveals himself through his journal entries as a modest, pleasant, eminently businesslike member of the middle class. He carefully notes train schedules, hotel arrangements, dates, food, and comments with naïve enthusiasm on the landscape, the local people, and the customs he encounters. Everything is normal, decent, even ordinary, characteristics which invest the account with what Otto might have described as the rational element that surrounds reality and structures it.

Despite the sanity and objectivity of these passages, Stoker mingles subtle hints of the numinous, or nonrational. As the train on which Harker travels reaches Budapest, he notes: "The impression I had was that we were leaving the West and entering the East; the most Western of splendid bridges over the Danube, which is here of noble width and depth, took us among the traditions of Turkish rule."[6] A feeling of something akin to wonder emerges as Harker penetrates this region of eastern Europe, suggesting that the rational and the nonrational are symbolized in terms of West and East, respectively.

Harker has read up on the region in the British Museum and notes its curious racial mix: "The section of Rumania is composed of Saxons, Dacians, Magyars, and Skeleys, the latter of whom are descended from the Huns." Unable to "light upon any map or work giving the exact locality of the Castle Dracula," Harker has discovered that it is set "on the borders of Transylvania, Moldavia, and Bukovina, in the midst of the Carpathian Mountains, one of the wildest and least known portions of Europe." These mysterious hints and suggestions are pointed up when he adds,

> I read that every known superstition in the world is gathered into the horseshoe of the Carpathians, as if it were the center of some sort of imaginative whirlpool; if so, my stay may be very interesting. (Mem., I must ask the Count all about them.)

At a hotel in Klausenburgh, where he spends the night, he notes:

> I did not sleep well, though my bed was comfortable enough, for I had all sorts of queer dreams. There was a dog howling all night under my window which may have had something to do with it; or it may have been the paprika, for I had to drink up all the water in my carafe, and was still thirsty.[7]

The accumulating sense of *mysterium* registers on Harker as he penetrates farther into this alien region. At the Golden Krone Hotel in Bistritz, the "cheery-looking woman" who greets him delivers a letter from Count Dracula, welcoming Harker to "my beautiful land"; but Harker grows apprehensive when the landlord pretends that he cannot speak German and his wife rather histrionically crosses herself and insists on giving Harker a rosary. There is irony (almost humor) in Harker's British imperturbability when confronted with these ominous tokens. The following day, as he travels by coach toward the Borgo Pass, where he is to meet his mysterious client, Harker notices the peasants making the sign against the evil eye and murmuring *vrolok* and *viboslak* ("werewolf" or "vampire"); but he merely notes: "Mem. I must ask the Count about these superstitions."[8]

As the carriage proceeds on its way, Harker is entranced by the sublime mountain scenery but cannot escape a growing sense of unease.

> As the evening fell it began to get very cold, and the growing twilight seemed to merge into one dark mistiness the gloom of the trees, oak, beech, and pine, though in the valleys which ran deep between the spurs of the hills . . . the dark firs stood out.

The road grows steep, the passengers in the carriage become excited, and at last, at the entrance to the Borgo Pass, Dracula's carriage appears. After one of the passengers quotes a line from Burger's "Lenore" ("For the dead travel fast"), Harker at last succumbs to the sense of *mysterium,* commenting: "I felt a strange chill and a lonely feeling come over me."[9]

It is notable that up to this point everything has been kept within the established boundaries of the natural, or rational. After Harker is transferred to Dracula's coach, however, the sense of the nonrational manifests itself with increasing intensity. As the coach pursues its steep ascent to the castle, Count Dracula displays his preternatural powers by dispersing a pack of wolves that menace the coach and by locating a treasure trove by means of the *blume falem*—the magical flame that appears on the eve of St. George. These clear signs of occult activity increase the conflict between rational and nonrational that grips Harker; but he persists in his determined resolve to ignore anything that threatens his sane, rational outlook.

Nonetheless, once he is within the walls of Dracula's castle, Harker's defenses begin to crumble. Like other "haunted castles" in Gothic literature, this castle stands as a symbol of the *mysterium tremendum*. In the exciting scenes that follow, Stoker intensifies the sense of the numinous and establishes its cosmic dimensions in the tale. To better understand the idea Stoker is projecting in this section of the tale, we must refer again to an important passage in *The Idea of the Holy* in which Otto works out the implications of what he calls "negative numinous." This passage, which appears in a long footnote, is only a suggestion of a concept Otto referred to several times but never satisfactorily explained. There is enough, however, to indicate that had he lived he might have provided a finished metaphysic of the "negative numinous."

The "ferocity" is the origin of Lucifer, in whom the mere potentiality of evil is actualized. It might be said that Lucifer is "fury," the hypostatized, the *mysterium tremendum* cut loose from the other elements and intensified to *mysterium horrendum*. The roots at least of this may be found in the Bible and the early Church. The ideas of propitiation and ransom are not without reference to Satan as well as to the divine wrath. The rationalism of the myth of the "fallen angel" does not render satisfactorily the horror of Satan and of the "depths of satan" (Rev. 2:24) and the "mystery of iniquity" (Thess. 2:7). It is a horror that is in some sort numinous, and we might designate the object of it as the negatively numinous. This also holds good of other religions than that of the Bible. In all religions, "the devilish" plays its part and has its place as that which, opposed to the divine, has yet something in common with it. As such it should be the subject of a special inquiry, which must be an analysis of fundamental feelings, and something very different from a mere record of the "evolution of the idea of the devil."[10]

Otto's concept of the "negative numinous" finds a striking embodiment in the character of Dracula. Though inimical to all evidence of the divine (he cringes with horror at Jonathan Harker's rosary), he nevertheless shares certain aspects of the divine power, for example, the ability to change his shape, become invisible, and read thoughts at a distance. Similarly, his lust for blood is a kind of propitiation of the dark forces he is leagued with as he seeks to evangelize the world to this ominous religion. Moreover, the mysterious laws that govern his activities are related to the divine. When he learns that Harker's law firm has purchased for him a large, ancient manor house in England with an antique chapel on its grounds, he says: "I rejoice that there is a chapel of old time. We Transylvanian nobles love not to think that our bones may be amongst the common dead."[11]

Such negative religious aspects of Dracula extend to his castle, his class, and to Transylvania itself. "We are in Transylvania," he tells Harker, echoing biblical language, "and Transylvania is not England. Our ways are not your ways, and there shall be to you many strange things." As the story continues it becomes evident that England and Transylvania stand as archetypes of the known in contrast to the unknown, the rational to the nonrational. "I long to go through the crowded streets of your mighty London," Dracula says, "to be in the midst of the whirl and rush of humanity, to share its life, its change, its death, and all that makes it what it is."[12]

Throughout the book Stoker surrounds Dracula with an aura of legendary associations. He seems to personify the East, with its mystery, as opposed to the orderly, rational bourgeois life of the West. The feeling is reinforced by Dracula's numerous references to his race:

We Szekelys have a right to be proud for in our veins flows the blood of many brave races who fought as the lion fights for lordship. Here, in the whirlpool of European races, the Ugric tribe bore down from Iceland the fighting spirit which Thor and Wodin gave them, which their Berserkers displayed to such fell intent. . . . Here too when they came they found the Huns, whose warlike fury had swept the earth like a living flame, till the dying peoples held that in their veins ran the blood of those old witches who, expelled from Sycthia, had mated with the devil in the desert. Fools, fools! What devil or what witch was ever so great as Attila, whose blood is in these veins?[13]

In these and other passages Stoker incorporates both legendary and historical elements, thus imbuing the story with a cosmic dimension. He reinforces this dimension with the character of Dracula himself. Dracula is apparently based on the historical figure of Vlad Tepes, a voivoide (or ruler) of Wallachia from 1456 to 1462, who must rank as one of history's bloodiest tyrants. His favorite method of execution was impalement, which he often witnessed with sadistic delight. "There was impalement from above—feet upwards—and impalement from below—head upwards; or through the heart or navel. There were nails in people's heads, maiming of limbs, blinding, strangulation, burning, the cutting of noses and ears."[14]

One of Stoker's imaginative triumphs in the novel is his synthesis of the vampire legend in the person of Vlad Tepes, who was known as Dracula (son of the Devil). By means of this central ideogram, Stoker was able to draw together racial, geographic, and cosmic notes and fuse them into a striking image of the "the daemonic." In *The Idea of the Holy,* Otto returns several times to a discussion of the daemonic element. A striking exhibition of it, he says, is seen in some remarks by Goethe, from which he quotes:

"The Daemonic is that which cannot be accounted for by understanding and reason. It chooses for itself obscure times

of darkness. . . . In a plain, prosaic town like Berlin it would
hardly find an opportunity to manifest itself. . . ."

"Does not the daemonic (asks Eckermann) also appear
in events?" "Pre-eminently so," said Goethe, "and as-
suredly in all which we cannot explain by intellect or reason.
And in general it is manifested throughout nature, visible
and invisible, in the most diverse ways. Many creatures in
the animal kingdom are of a wholly daemonic kind, and in
many we see some aspect of the daemonic operative."[15]

Goethe's remarks may explain the association of the vampire with bats, wolves, and rats. Similarly, the daemonic is
associated with such qualities as energy, fury, implacable
hatred, and a general "overpoweringness." The daemonic,
says Goethe, was manifested in Napoleon, a

daemonic character [which] appears in its most dreadful
form when it stands out dominatingly in some *man*. Such
are not always the most remarkable men, either in spiritual
quality or natural talents, and they seldom have any goodness of heart to recommend them. But an incredible force
goes forth from them, and they exercise incredible power
over all creatures, nay, perhaps even over the elements. And
who can say how far such an influence may extend?[16]

The preternatural powers with which Stoker invests his
vampire are aspects of the daemonic. Like the monster in
Mary Shelley's *Frankenstein*, Dracula is symbolically associated with darkness, slyness, cruelty, and fierce egotism.
Like the monster, he commits various atrocities, although
these seem at times like mere means to ends; for his ultimate
goal is to establish and maintain himself in opposition to
that sacred power in which he indirectly participates.

After Harker's escape from the castle, the setting of the
novel changes to England, where Dracula, bringing with
him his coffins of sacred earth, has established himself at

his estate of Carfax. This change of scene is used to introduce a new ontological tension into the story. England, as we have already seen, is the polar opposite of Transylvania and the East. It is the rational center of the novel, the realm of reason, science, practicality, order, common sense.

To carry out this idea, Stoker assembles in England a cast of characters who, in one way or another, are all representatives of the rational. This small group of people, who become Dracula's opponents, are members of the bourgeoisie, with its norms of respectability, hard work, probity, and good sense. As a consequence, they are deliberately depicted as "type characters" but in the best sense of the term. Stoker distinguishes each character by a strongly individualistic touch. For example, Lucy Westenra, Dracula's first victim, is a charming, if slightly idealized, picture of Victorian femininity: witty, intelligent, romantic. On the other hand, Mina Murray, Lucy's confidante and former schoolmate, is practical and ambitious. Lacking Lucy's inherited wealth, she has trained herself as an expert stenographer and dreams of aiding her fiancé, Jonathan Harker, when he returns to assume his duties as a solicitor.

The male characters are sketched with equally broad but convincing strokes. Lord Godalming, generous and dependable, displays the better qualities of the British upper class. John Seward, a psychiatrist, is cool, resourceful, scientific. Even Quincy Morris, the plucky, faintly comic American who joins the group, is, within the context of the novel's action, convincing enough. Although Morris speaks a rather absurd, and often criticized, variety of American slang, Stoker drops hints suggesting that this is an ironic pose intended to amuse his English friends. Obviously, these characters are not intended by Stoker as fully developed characterizations but rather as sharply etched representatives of the rational structure surrounding the occult, or the nonrational, elements of the narrative.

The scene of action during most of the long middle section of the novel is the area around London and the nearby town of Purfleet, where John Seward owns and operates a sanitarium for the mentally ill. Through something more than coincidence, the grounds of the asylum adjoin Carfax Manor, the ancient, decaying estate Dracula has purchased and to which his coffins are transported. In choosing this setting Stoker again provides a highly effective ideogram for the numinous, since an asylum, or madhouse, suggests the scientific and the rational, on the one hand, and the alien and the nonrational, on the other.

It is, in fact, a simple step for Stoker to transpose the events at the asylum into the realm of the supernatural. This is readily seen in the character of Renfield, one of the patients at the sanitarium, who is secretly in league with Dracula. Not only does the character Renfield serve to introduce a note of ghastly humor into the story, he links the events at the sanitarium with Dracula as well.[17]

When introduced, Renfield suffers from an obscure form of mania that causes him to collect flies, spiders, and sparrows, about which he keeps a meticulous record in a notebook. The secret of his delusion is his lust for blood, which Dracula has promised to satisfy in return for his services. The quasi-religious nature of his delusion is evident when Dracula draws near the asylum and Renfield's manic delight in insects suddenly disappears.

"What?" Seward asks. "You don't mean to tell me you don't care about spiders?"

To which Renfield replies in biblical language:

"The bride-maidens rejoice the eyes that wait the coming of the bride; but when the bride draweth nigh, then the maidens shine not to the eyes that are filled."[18]

Renfield's curious lapses from maniacal strength to passivity, and his abrupt changes from the wildest insanity to the most lucid self-possession exemplify the rational-nonrational paradigm that infuses the story.

At this point, Stoker introduces the final ideogramic element in his tale, in the person of the Belgian physician, Dr. Abraham Van Helsing. Van Helsing's aid is requested when Seward and Lucy's other friends realize that in their struggle against Dracula they are out of their depth. Their efforts, especially those of Seward, are based on science and other rational means; but these prove ineffective. Paradoxically, it is Seward the scientist who grasps the idea that science alone is not sufficient. As a consequence, he calls on his old mentor, Van Helsing. "He is a seemingly arbitrary man," Seward explains; "but this is because he knows what he is talking about better than anyone else. He is a philosopher and a metaphysician, and one of the most advanced scientists of his day." Van Helsing now assumes the role of Dracula's chief adversary. Moreover, he takes on the character of an ideogramic figure in the novel. He is best understood as the Jungian archetypes "the wise old man" and "the cosmic man."

That there is a connection between the Jungian archetypes and Otto's conception of the numinous is clear from statements made by Jung, who was well acquainted with Otto's writings. In *Psychology and Religion,* Jung concedes:

Religion, as the Latin word denotes, is a careful and scrupulous observation of what Rudolf Otto aptly termed the "numinosum," that is, a dynamic existence or effect, not caused by an arbitrary act of the will. . . . The numinosum is either a quality of a visible object or the influence of a visible or an invisible presence causing a peculiar alteration of consciousness.[19]

The relationship between the Jungian archetypes and the

numinous is set forth by Jung: "when an archetype appears in a dream, in a fantasy, or in life, it always brings with it a certain influence or power by virtue of which it either exercises a numinous or fascinating effect or impels to action."[20]

Of the archetypes Jung collected in his various studies of human consciousness, two seem closely related to Stoker's novel: "the wise old man" (cosmic man) and "the demon." The demon is an aspect of what Jung called the "shadow" archetype, the dark, hidden portion of the personality. Curiously, it is related to that of "the wise old man," a benevolent, sagacious type suggesting the complete development Jung called "individuation":

> One of the archetypes that is almost invariably met with in the projection of unconscious collective contents is the "magic demon" with mysterious powers. . . . The image of this demon forms one of the lowest and most ancient states in the conception of God. It is the type of primitive tribal sorcerer or medicine-man, a peculiarly gifted personality endowed with magical powers. This figure often appears as dark-skinned and of mongoloid type, and then it represents a negative and possibly dangerous aspect. Sometimes it can hardly be distinguished, if at all, from the shadow; but the more the thematical note predominates, the easier it is to make the distinction, and this is not without relevance insofar as the demon can also have a very positive aspect as "the wise old man."[21]

In *Dracula* these related but distinct ideograms are personified in the vampire and his implacable antagonist Van Helsing. Dracula—"dark-skinned and of mongoloid type . . . negative . . . possibly dangerous"—represents the *demon,* an aspect of the cosmic man that embodies the profane, or negative, aspect of the numinous. Van Helsing, Dracula's equal in power, determination, and occult knowledge, evinces the benign (or sacred) elements of the numinous. Stoker, in fact, has drawn what would seem to be a series of conscious parallels between the two; both come from foreign countries and speak with distinctly awkward accents, and both, in turn, can be imperious, arbitrary, and crafty.

There are differences, however. With his plain, Belgian respectability and bourgeois cast of mind, Van Helsing typifies an orderly, rational pattern that even at times contains humor. His Belgian accent, which one critic[22] calls "delicatessen Dutch," is used deliberately to suggest the faintly risible overtones of his character, as in the well-known speech concerning King Laugh. Although he is a celebrated scientist, his view of life is strongly conservative, or traditional, and while he is on occasion stern and arbitrary, he is by nature kindly, even avuncular.

Dracula manifests many of the same characteristics but perverts them into a malign parody of the sacred. He possesses no humor yet is capable of a queer irony. His smile is described as "cruel," and he often sneers. His accent, as clumsy as that of Van Helsing, carries no comic overtones but rather hints at a kind of alien poetry. When the wolves howl about his castle, he tells Harker: "Listen to them—the children of the night. What music they make! . . . you dwellers in the city cannot enter into the feelings of the hunter."[23]

The physical appearances of the two contrast strikingly. Dracula's face is

> strong—very strong—aquiline, with high bridge of the thin nose and peculiarly arched nostrils, with lofty domed forehead, and hair growing scantily round the temples, but profusely elsewhere. . . . His eyebrows were very massive, almost meeting over the nose. . . . The mouth, so far as I could see it under the heavy mustache, was fixed and rather cruel-looking with peculiarly white teeth that protruded over the lips.

He has "pointed ears," and the entire face gives an impression of pallor. He is tall, cadaverous, and dresses in black.[24]

Van Helsing, on the other hand, is of medium height, strongly built, and deep-chested. His head is "noble, well-sized, broad and large behind the ears." He is clean-shaven, and his face is large and square with "a mobile mouth, good-sized nose . . . and big bushy brows." His hair is red, and his blue eyes are "widely set apart and are quick and tender or stern with the man's moods."[25]

The impression in each case is one of power but power arising from opposite sources. Although Van Helsing is a notable scientist, he realizes that science is powerless against Dracula and for help turns to his deeply held Catholic faith and to white magic. Dracula, by contrast, employs *black* magic.

The struggle between these two "cosmic men" forms the central portion of the story.[26] This conflict is deepened by Stoker's artistic incorporation of the many legends and beliefs concerning vampires. Stoker's strategy in employing this material coincides with the "rational versus nonrational" pattern we saw above. By structuring the story on a firmly realistic basis and introducing as his protagonist a man of impeccable scientific background, Stoker conjures the reader into accepting the marvelous. This strategy is clearly pointed up in an interesting speech by Van Helsing:

> To believe in things that you cannot. Let me illustrate. I once heard of an American who so defined faith, "that which enables us to believe things which we know to be untrue." For one, I follow that man. He meant that we shall have an open mind, and not let a little bit of truth check the rush of a big truth, like a small rock does a railway truck. We get the small truth first. Good! We keep him, and we value him; but all the same we must not let him think himself all the truth in the universe.[27]

Despite its humorous overtones, the epistemological basis of the speech is clear enough. It continues as Van Helsing expounds the history of vampirism:

> All we have to go upon are traditions and superstitions. These do not at the first appear much, when the matter is one of life and death—nay, of more than either life or death. Yet we must be satisfied. . . . Take it, then, that the vampire and the belief in his limitations and his cure, rest for the moment on the same base. For let me tell you he is known everywhere that men have been. In old Greece, in old Rome; he flourish in Germany all over, in France, in India, even in the Chersonese; and in China. . . . He have follow the wake of the berserker, Icelander, the devil-begotten Hun, the Slav, the Saxon, the Magyar.[28]

The recitation of racial and geographical names, reminiscent of earlier speeches by Dracula, serves to infuse the story with a sense of cosmic action. As the struggle between these two cosmic men continues, it is lifted above the rational elements of the tale into a region of dread and wonder. Historical traditions, legends, and occult lore give the book a quality that must be considered epic.

In the concluding section of the novel, Stoker faced the somewhat difficult task of sustaining this intense level of numinous feeling. Having been irrevocably defeated in England, Dracula now attempts to return to his castle in the Carpathians. Because he retains a degree of occult influence over Mina Harker, however, he must be pursued and extirpated by Van Helsing and his group.[29] They follow Dracula back to his native Transylvania, which, as we have seen, is the focal point of the novel's nonrational forces. The cyclical pattern is now complete, with the rational forces of the West in pursuit of the nonrational East.[30] But a new element has been added. In the opening section of the novel, Jonathan

Harker, as representative of the bourgeois West, comes equipped with the ineffective powers of civilization. Now, under the tutelage of Van Helsing, the group understands the preternatural elements they face. They have been initiated into the cosmic pattern of the sacred and are able to deal with the counterforces of the profane. Thus, "When we find the habitation of this man-that-was," Van Helsing explains,

> we can confine him to the coffin and destroy him. We obey what we know. But he is clever. I have asked my friend Arminius, of Buda-Pesth University, to make his record; and from all the means that are, he tells me of what he has been. He must, indeed, have been that Voivoide Dracula who won his name against the Turk, over the great river on the very frontier of Turkey-land. . . . In the records are such words as "stregoica"—witch, "ordog" and "pokol"— Satan and hell; and in one manuscript this very Dracula is spoke of as a "vampyr." . . . There have been from the loins of this very one great men and good women, and their graves make sacred the earth where alone this foulness can dwell. For it is not the least of its terrors that this evil thing is rooted deep in all good; in soil barren of holy memories it cannot rest.[31]

In the chase sequences that bring the novel to its exciting conclusion, Stoker retains control over the fugitive emotions he deals with by grounding the action in a firmly realistic context. As Van Helsing and his group return to the East, they encounter the same small difficulties and obstacles that Harker faced in the novel's opening passages. Details of luggage, train schedules, lodging, and conflicts with local officials keep the narrative firmly in place against a background increasingly mysterious. When at last the travelers reach Transylvania and the vicinity of Dracula's castle, the effect is one of a great cloud slowly being lifted. The exotic geography of the region—its mountains, stately rivers, half-civilized people, wolves, gypsies, and the great castle itself[32]—come into weird, faintly disturbing focus, as though one were remembering a dream. The writing takes on a fifth-dimensional quality, as seen in the following passage from Mina Harker's diary:

> When we had gone about a mile, I was tired with the heavy walking and sat down to rest. Then we looked back and saw where the clear line of Dracula's castle cut the sky; for we were so deep under the hill whereon it was set that the angle of perspective of the Carpathian Mountains was far below it. We saw it in all its grandeur perched a thousand feet on the summit of a sheer precipice, and with seemingly a great gap between it and the steep of the adjacent mountain on any side. There was something wild and uncanny about the place. We could hear the distant howling of wolves.[33]

This exciting coda, culminating in the savage ritual of Dracula's extinction, has a theatrical quality about it that is reminiscent of Poe:

> The sun was almost down on the mountain tops, and the shadows of the whole group fell upon the snow. I saw the Count lying within the box upon the earth, some of which the rude falling from the cart had scattered over him. He was deathly pale, just like a waxen image, and the red eyes glared with the horrible vindictive look which I knew too well.
>
> As I looked, the eyes saw the sinking sun, and the look of hate in them turned to triumph.
>
> But on the instant, came the sweep and flash of Jonathan's great knife. I shrieked as I saw it shear through the throat; whilst at the same moment, Mr. Morris's bowie knife plunged into the heart. . . .
>
> The Castle of Dracula now stood out against the red sky,

and every stone of its broken battlements was articulated against the light of the setting sun.[34]

The firm prose of the final scenes adds the note of credibility the reader needs in order to accept the lurid events. As is true of all masters of prose narrative, Stoker's sense of proportion and balance never deserts him. He retains the feeling of realism—uppermost in writing of this kind—until the final words, structuring the numinous emotion in a context of versimilitude. The reader puts the book down and returns to the real world with the distinct feeling of having glimpsed a deeper reality underlying the various marvels encountered in *Dracula*.

8

The Modern Period

The efflorescence of the ghostly tale that marked the end of the Victorian period was followed by a declining interest in the genre during the early years of the present century. The reasons for such a decline may lie in the proliferation of new movements in the arts and sciences. In mainstream literature it was an age of experimentation, with Eliot, Yeats, Joyce, Virginia Woolf, and others pursuing new forms of poetry and fiction; in science, politics, and economics, the period was one of intellectual ferment, of discovery and new departures. In such a milieu the supernatural tale, like certain other forms of literature, was perhaps crowded out.

Whatever the reason, there was a thinness of production, with only a few first-rate writers devoting themselves exclusively to numinous themes. Among these the most original, and in many ways most interesting, was Arthur Machen (1863–1947), a Welsh writer of occult tales whose work enjoyed a considerable vogue in the years around the turn of the century. The son of a clergyman, Machen was born at Caerlon, Wales, the site of an early Roman military establishment in Britain. As a boy he wandered the hills and woods of this picturesque region, absorbing the traditions of King Arthur, the Romans, and the elves and fairies—the "Little People," as he later called them. After an irregular education he went to London and entered journalism. In the 1890s he began a series of occult tales that made him famous.[1]

Like Eliot, Yeats, and Joyce, Machen was interested in mythological themes. Like them, he created his "private" myth, one combining the gods of Greece and Rome with the legends of the "little people" of his native Welsh hills. But the little people of Machen's stories are in no wise the charming creatures of later folklore; they are a malign race, akin to pagan nature gods, who have "gone underground" in order to perpetuate their existence despite the impact of modern civilization.[2] Most of the tales show these dark, shadowy creatures emerging in modern Wales, a region Machen depicts with authenticity and charm.

The unique, numinous quality of Machen's work derives from this juxtaposition of rational and nonrational elements: the normal, unsuspecting life of the modern town and the countryside infiltrated by the uncanny "powers" of the past. The plots and characters of the tales frequently are bizarre and sometimes unhealthy. Machen was a close friend of A. E. Waite, a well-known occultist of the time. He was also a member of the notorious Order of the Golden Dawn, the occultist society to which Yeats belonged.[3] Through such channels Machen rediscovered the ancient feeling for magic and the preternatural. With the exception of Matthew Lewis, no writer of Gothic fiction seems closer than Machen to the feeling-state Rudolf Otto describes as the "negative numinous." Despite this disturbing, all-too-real portrayal of the occult, Machen's work is infused with a subtle poetic quality that redeems its unsavory elements.[4]

Machen's best-known work is *The Great God Pan,* a novelette typical of his work, both for its poetic power and for its incredible plot and occasionally horrifying details. The horrific incidents in the story, which might seem mere bad taste in another context, are deliberate with Machen and are used to produce the sense of "daemonic dread (c.f. the horror of Pan)" that Otto speaks of when describing the sense of fear (the *tremendum*) in numinous feeling:

> It is this feeling which, emerging in the mind of primeval man, forms the starting-point for the entire religious development in history. "Daemons" and "gods" alike spring from this root, and all the products of "mythological apperception."[5]

The underlying sense of horror in the narrative is built on a pseudo-scientific premise somewhat reminiscent of *Frankenstein.* A Welsh physician, Dr. Raymond, has discovered an operation on the brain ("a slight lesion in the grey matter") that will produce a "lifting of the veil" from human consciousness. As a result of the operation, its victim—a young Welsh girl—enters a twilight zone of human consciousness in which she meets and mingles with the powers of antiquity, notably the great god Pan. As in *Frankenstein,* this basically incredible situation is worked up with surprising touches of poetry, touches that evoke a feeling of primitive wonder on the part of the reader. " 'You may think all this strange nonsense,' the physician remarks to a friend. 'It may be strange, but it is true, and the ancients knew what lifting the veil means. They called it seeing the god Pan.' "[6]

As a result of the young girl's meeting with Pan, the god conceives an avatar—a beautiful but amoral woman named Helen Vaughan. In the remainder of the tale this demigoddess is shown spreading a web of evil over the quiet Welsh countryside and later in London, where she corrupts a series of lovers who are driven to suicide. Many of the subsequent incidents are bizarre, grotesque, and appalling (Edwardian readers thought them "shocking"); but Machen's unfailing instinct for the daemonic shapes this variegated material into something like organic unity. In one instance, a London artist named Meyrick, who has fallen victim to Helen Vaughan's "charms," leaves behind a collection of drawings which are later discovered by his friend, Villiers.

> Villiers turned page after page, absorbed, in spite of himself, in the frightful Walpurgis Night of evil, strange monstrous evil, that the dead artist had set forth in hard black and white. The figures of Fauns and Satyrs and Ægipans danced before his eyes, the darkness of the thicket, the dance on the mountaintop, the scenes by lonely shores, in green vineyards, by rocks and desert places, passed before him: a world before which the human soul seemed to shrink back and shudder.[7]

The incantatory quality of these passages, which has influenced later writers, arises from the strain of "daemonism" Otto notes as the first perception of the numinous in primitive religions. Machen seems particularly adept at assembling the notes of this antique feeling. As the passage suggests, the satyrs, fauns, Ægipans, darkness of the thicket, and loneliness of desert places add up to that "shudder" ancient man felt when confronted by the mystery of the gods.

In addition to the daemonic, Machen excels in depicting "horror," a quality Otto found in primitive notions of *clean* and *unclean,* which result later in the numinous sense of the sacred and the profane. In the conclusion of *The Great*

God Pan, Helen Vaughan's suicide results in the following loathsome transformation, which is witnessed and later recounted by a London physician, Dr. Robert Matheson:

> I saw the form waver from sex to sex, dividing itself from itself, and then again reunited. Then I saw the body descend to the beasts from whence it ascended, and that which was on the heights go down to the depths, even to the abyss of all being.
>
> I watched, and at last I saw nothing but a substance as jelly. Then the ladder was ascended again. . . . for one instant I saw a Form, shaped in dimness before me, which I will not further describe. But the symbol of this form may be seen in ancient sculptures, and in paintings which survived beneath the lava, too foul to be spoken of.[8]

A comment from Otto's *Idea of the Holy* may help explain such curious and appalling elements in Machen's work:

> Between this [feeling of disgust] and the feeling of the "horrible" there is a very close analogy; and from this it becomes apparent, in accordance with the law of reciprocal attraction between analogous feelings and emotions, how the "natural" unclean or impure is bound to pass over into, and develop in, the sphere of the numinous.[9]

Such prereligious factors appear constantly in Machen's work, giving it a unique sense of the numinous. His strange and disturbing harmonies, though somewhat esoteric, have gained him a secure place in the annals of supernatural fiction.[10]

A writer of equal power and artistry in the period under discussion is Algernon Blackwood (1869–1951). Blackwood, a British author who emigrated to Canada early in his life, is the acknowledged master of supernatural tales of nature and the out-of-doors. The settings of his stories, rendered with unsurpassed authenticity, include lonely stretches of Canadian wilderness, desolate marshes of the upper Danube, and remote islands off the coast of northern Europe. Though not mythic in the sense of Machen's tales, many of these stories suggest a related feeling-state, namely, the sense of haunted presence that primitive man must have associated with sacred groves, mountains, streams, and other impressive natural objects.[11]

The central impulse of Blackwood's stories clearly is related to what Otto describes as the feeling of "haunted places." "There is none of us," Otto says, "who has any living capacity for emotion but must have known at some time or at some place what it is to feel really 'Uncanny,' to have a feeling of 'eeriness.' " This feeling rises spontaneously in the mind and sometimes attaches itself to no particular object or being but rather to the surroundings.

> If in this implicit form it is summed up in a phrase, this will be merely some such exclamation as "How uncanny!" or "How eerie is this place." If the feeling becomes explicit it generally takes a negative form: "It is not quite right here. . . ." The English "This place is haunted" shows a transition to a positive form of expression.[12]

Such obscure feelings may on occasion become explicit recognition of a transcendent Something, "a real operative entity of a numinous kind, which later, as the development proceeds, assumes concrete form as a 'numen loci,' a daemon, an 'ell,' a 'Baal,' or the like." The German expression *Es spukt hier* (literally, "it haunts here") is an offshoot of this same primary emotion. We can, Otto says, recapture the numinous sense of these words as they apply to "aweful," "holy," or numen-possessed places.[13]

These remarks shed light on Blackwood's unique ability to recapture the emotion Otto describes. In Blackwood's best stories it is the numinous landscape or background that dominates; the human actors, perhaps to the bewilderment of certain readers, fill a subsidiary role.

A good example of this peculiar power is seen in Blackwood's best-known story, "The Willows." In the opening passages, the unidentified narrator—probably a young Englishman—and his morose Swedish companion proceed on a canoe trip into the upper reaches of the Danube, where, amid a lonely, remote marshland they come upon a small island entirely covered by willow trees. They make camp, prepare a meal, and carry out other ordinary tasks; but as night falls, an odd and seemingly alien emotion is aroused in the narrator by the willow-covered island.

> Great revelations of nature, of course, never fail to impress in one way or another, and I was no stranger to moods of the kind. Mountains overawe and oceans terrify, while the mystery of great forests exercises a spell peculiarly its own. But all these, at one point or another, somewhere link on intimately with human life and human experience. They stir comprehensible, even if alarming, emotions. They tend on the whole to exalt.
>
> With this multitude of willows, however, it was something far different, I felt. Some essence emanated from them that besieged the heart. A sense of awe awakened, true, but of awe touched somewhere by a vague terror.[14]

Here, Blackwood explicitly differentiates the sublime from the numinous (in accordance with what Otto called the "association of feelings"). He locates this force, or power, in the landscape itself. The feeling aroused is similar to those mysterious emanations of sacred groves in Roman religion, for example, the "talking trees" of the *Aeneid*. Herbert Jennings Rose, an authority on ancient Roman religion, says of this feeling:

> The Romans . . . believed in a supernatural power or influ-
> ence which they called *numen*. . . . Until the time of Augus-
> tus it [was] never used to mean any personal or individual
> god. . . . Even inanimate things, if there is something holy
> or uncanny about them, may have, or even be, *numen*.[15]

As the tale continues, this perception becomes explicit in
the narrator's mind:

> The psychology of places for some imaginations at least, is
> very vivid; for the wanderer, especially, camps have their
> "note" whether of welcome or rejection. . . . And the note
> of this willow-camp now became unmistakably plain to me:
> we were interlopers, trespassers; we were not welcomed.
> The sense of unfamiliarity grew upon me as I stood there
> watching.[16]

The next day, the feeling of threat from the island and the
willows is focused on a series of magical events. The narrator
sees—or thinks he sees—enormous shapes moving within
the branches of the trees, and each morning the willows
appear to have moved closer to the tent. The canoe and its
paddle are mysteriously damaged, effectively trapping the
two men on the island. In addition, they discover strange
patterns in the sand around their tent: basin-shaped inden-
tations that vary in depth and size from that of a teacup to
a large bowl.

These accumulating notes of the nonrational induce a
feeling of hysteria in the Swede, who mutters vaguely of
"forces" surrounding them, producing disorder and destruction. The narrator attempts to rationalize these growing
fears, but eventually he too succumbs to them. The island
and surrounding area, he concludes, have become the focal
point for powers or influences that have "leaked through"
from some dimension "beyond." The frontiers of this un-

known world impinge on our world in the area of the camp; and the uncanny phenomena the two men have witnessed are evidence that the powers of this unknown dimension are groping about searching for them. It becomes clear, in fact, that they are to be the sacrificial victims of these powers.

In the frightening conclusion of the story, the two are "saved" by the appearance of the body of a peasant who drowned during the storm and whose body washed up on the island, thus providing a vicarious sacrifice. At dawn the two companions find his body in the sand with "Their mark. . . . Their awful mark!" upon it:

> just as the body swung round to the current the face and the exposed chest turned full towards us, and showed plainly how the skin and flesh were indented with small hollows, beautifully formed, and exactly similar in shape and kind to the sandfunnels that we had found all over the island.[17]

The work of Machen and Blackwood added new, distinct notes to the numinous tale, the first by means of a "mythological" dimension and the second by infusing the genre with a sense of "haunted place." A third writer of the period, one who benefited from the work of both men, was H. P. Lovecraft (1890–1937).[18] Lovecraft, who has become something of a cult figure for modern devotees of supernatural fiction, makes an interesting case study of numinous literature, since he was a self-proclaimed scientific materialist. Although he denied the reality of the supernatural, he used his impressive literary powers to depict it, thus demonstrating that Otto's concept cuts across numerous philosophical lines of thought.

Lovecraft was born and spent most of his life in Providence, Rhode Island. A virtual recluse, he eked out a precarious living as, ironically, a ghost writer. His own work appeared mostly in pulp magazines of the day, notably

Weird Tales and *Amazing Stories*. Despite the neglect he received during his lifetime his stories have increasingly gained scholarly recognition since his death.[19]

Because his work contains major strengths combined with certain peculiarities, which may or may not be considered weaknesses depending on the point of view, Lovecraft's eventual position as a writer of Gothic tales is difficult to assess. In Edmund Wilson's view, he is little more than a hack; to T. O. Mabbott, he is a gifted amateur; whereas to the Lovecraft enthusiast, his work ranks with that of Poe.[20] Despite these differences of opinion, it seems fairly clear that Lovecraft's work will be a source of interest for years to come.

Most of Lovecraft's tales and novelettes are set in New England, a region he knew intimately and one he depicts with a realism surprising in such a reclusive figure. Various representative New England types, drawn with a charm reminiscent of Hawthorne, populate the stories. Like Faulkner's Yoknapatawpha series, Lovecraft's tales are related to one another by fictional towns and institutions—Dunwich, Innsmouth, Kingsport, Miskatonic University—which correspond to real places.

The ability to create a literary world of his own led Lovecraft to concoct a numinous mythology which came to be known as the "Cthulhu mythos." "All my stories," he wrote in an often-quoted passage, "unconnected as they may be, are based on the fundamental lore or legend that this world was inhabited at one time by another race who, in practicing black magic, lost their foothold and were expelled, yet live on outside ever ready to take possession of this earth again."[21]

This bizarre conception is equalled by the bizarre names Lovecraft attaches to the gods of his pantheon: Azathoth, the blind idiot god; Yog-Sothoth, the "all-in-one and one-in-all"; Great Cthulhu, dweller in hidden R'lyeh; Shub-

Niggurath, and so on. The entire "mythic concept," which is a source of intense interest to the fan of Lovecraft writing, may seem somewhat artificial to the casual reader; but, given Lovecraft's impressive prose rhythms, erudition, and convincing realism, this mythic concept seems to work, at least in his best tales. A unique vision of numinous reality emerges, a world of weird colors and shapes, but one that is anchored firmly in the ordinary world.

The pattern of most of Lovecraft's tales differs from that of many of the writers discussed in this book. Whereas Henry James, Bram Stoker, Blackwood, and others begin with a carefully constructed background of rational events from which the nonrational emerges, Lovecraft's method is to plunge immediately into his material, combining fantastic hints of the occult with pedestrian details. The opening passage of one of his best stories, "The Colour Out of Space," provides a good example of this technique:

> West of Arkham the hills rise wild, and there are valleys with deep woods that no axe has ever cut. There are dark narrow glens where the trees slope fantastically, and where thin brooklets trickle without ever having caught the glint of sunlight. On the gentler slopes there are farms, ancient and rocky, with squat, moss-coated cottages brooding eternally over old New England secrets in the lee of great ledges; but these are all vacant now. . . .
>
> The old folks have gone away, and foreigners do not like to live there. . . . The place is not good for imagination, and does not bring restful dreams at night.[22]

Passages such as this, which reveal Lovecraft's admirable qualities as a prose stylist, are not hard to find in his work. His unfailing sense of rhythm, the exact yet poetic vocabulary, the clear-cut imagery, and especially the fantastic reach of his imagination entitle him to high rank in this regard. In addition, a wide and precise antiquarian knowledge of New England pervades Lovecraft's work. The architecture, history, and customs of his native region provide a realistic background for the nonrational atmosphere that broods over the tales. This element in his work has attracted numerous imitators, making the New England milieu a kind of stalking ground for modern Gothic writers.

As with other works of the supernatural, Lovecraft's stories show only minimal interest in character, motivation, and psychology. Lovecraft was a great admirer of eighteenth-century literature; in keeping with its norms, he sought to create *representative* types rather than strongly individualistic characters. He was a master of the art of representation, however, capable of summoning up type characters with swift, authentic touches. Indeed, his tales contain an impressive array of characters drawn from all segments of New England society: reclusive scholars, strange old mountain people from the hills of western Massachusetts, sea captains and sailors, professors from Miskatonic University, shy old spinsters living on their memories of the past, artists and writers, business people, physicians, and a considerable sampling of immigrants from Italy and the Orient.

This New England milieu, with its traditions and legends and faint effluvia of decadence, forms a fitting accompaniment to the supernatural machinery of Lovecraft's myth of elder gods and monsters. He once explained the theory behind this "cosmic myth" as follows:

> The "punch" of a truly weird tale is simply some violation or transcending of fixed cosmic law—an imaginative escape from palling reality—since phenomena rather than persons are the logical "heroes." Horrors should be original—the use of common myths and legends being a weakening influence.[23]

Lovecraft may have derived his idea of phenomena as hero from Blackwood; there can be little doubt that the cosmic myth was suggested by Machen's work.[24] Unlike either writer, though, Lovecraft shows a lack of reserve in depicting his frightful monsters and slimy creatures from outer space. The horrors are heaped up; the reader "sups full on horror." Moreover, the passages describing these numinous entities are worked up in a vocabulary of the outré. The following examples should suffice to make the point.

From *At the Mountains of Madness,* one reads of "that fetid, unglimpsed mountain of slime-spewing protoplasm whose race had conquered the abyss and sent land pioneers to re-carve and squirm through the burrows of the hills." In "The Call of Cthulhu," the monster is described as bursting forth "like smoke from its eon-long imprisonment, visibly darkening the sun as it slunk away into the shrunken and gibbous sky on flapping membranous wings."[25]

There is a naïve quality about these descriptions, occasionally reminiscent of the naïveté of the older Gothic novels, especially *The Castle of Otranto;* yet it is probably deliberate and, surprisingly enough, it often works. Perhaps the key to Lovecraft's power lies in his ability to arouse what Carl Jung might have called numinous archetypes of the collective unconscious.[26]

In his wide-ranging investigations Jung found recurring images of demons and monsters in the dreams and fantasies of his patients. These images, in turn, often corresponded with those he discovered in the religions and mythologies of primitive peoples. The correspondence between such archetypes was not, he thought, accidental; they were, in fact, transformed impressions of often-repeated experiences, and they were often numinous. "For when an archetype appears in a dream, in a fantasy, or in life," he wrote, "it always brings with it a certain influence or power by virtue of which it either exercises a numinous or a fascinating effect, or impels to action."[27]

Unlike Freud, who interpreted such material as sublimated sexuality, Jung accorded it an important place in man's spiritual life: "We should never identify ourselves with reason," he says; "for man is not and never will be a creature of reason alone, a fact to be noted by all pedantic culture-mongers. The irrational cannot be and must not be extirpated."[28] This, though overstating the matter slightly, may help explain the urgency of Lovecraft's nonrational visions and the fascination they hold for certain readers; for the gods of the "Cthulhu mythology" and the Jungian archetypes are both born of the impulse Otto called the *mysterium tremendum et fascinans.*[29]

The history of occult literature in modern times amounts to a virtual renaissance of the form and can be adequately compared to the phenomenon of the eighteenth-century Gothic novel. This sudden upsurge of interest in the "old sacred terror" has resulted in an unparalleled production of novels, tales, and literary studies of the genre. Publishers now vie for new titles, and a substantial number of the classics have been reissued. Similarly, the film and television industries have exploited the possibilities of the form, ransacking the castles, tombs, and cellars of occult fiction, searching for new apparitions to feed the public's appetite.

Inevitably, the quality of this relatively sudden outpouring is uneven; much of it is ephemeral and will go the way of similar eighteenth-century Gothics now of interest only to literary historians. Some of it, on the other hand, is worth reading, especially for its relationship to older traditions of occult literature. Among contemporary practitioners of the form, first place unquestionably belongs to Shirley Jackson, whose untimely death deprived the supernatural tale of its most distinguished talent since H. P. Lovecraft. Ira Levin's popular novel *Rosemary's Baby* is based on a premise similar to *The Great God Pan;* and William P. Blatty's *The Exorcist,* despite a generally deplorable style, contains passages suggesting the daemonic note of Matthew G. Lewis's *The Monk.* More recently, the work of Stephen King, Peter Straub, and Ramsey Campbell displays a sophisticated employment of techniques and themes developed by earlier masters of the genre, especially Henry James, Arthur Machen, and H. P. Lovecraft. Mention might also be made of T. E. D. Klein, whose recent novel, *The Ceremonies,* shows innate understanding of the numinous and gives promise of better things to come.

We are much too close in time to the modern supernatural tale to render final judgments, however. In a period of such intense activity as this, it is impossible to do more than keep up with general developments and make the broadest distinctions. The situation, though, is a cause for general rejoicing among devotees of ghostly literature. Among other things, it demonstrates that an age of technology and science cannot extinguish mankind's spiritual hunger. In spite of computers, genetic manipulation, and atomic energy, the quest for the numinous lives on.

9

Analyzing the
mysterium tremendum

In the preceding pages we have explored certain representative supernatural tales by means of Rudolf Otto's concept
of the numinous, the *mysterium tremendum et fascinans*.
My purpose has been to point out in Gothic fiction a kind
of ontological structure and, as a consequence, absolve it
from the charge of lacking moral depth and high seriousness. In analyzing this material I have tried as well to explain
some of the aesthetic principles writers in the genre have
employed in attempting to achieve their goal.

Although I have on occasion compared and contrasted
writers and periods, my method of surveying Gothic literature is mainly a chronological one. Such a method, I feel,
exhibits both the historical development of the numinous
and its universality. On the other hand, a chronological
survey often results in something less than an orderly arrangement of ideas. To obviate this, I want to conclude this
study by summing up the principles arrived at and discussing the objective value of the numinous experience.

In Chapter 1, I describe the ghostly tale as presenting the reader with an "ontological challenge." Such a challenge, if accepted, draws the reader into a dimension of reality that lies beyond the boundaries of ordinary experience. One of the most recurrent examples of this challenge in supernatural literature turns on the distinction Otto draws between rational and nonrational experience. By the *rational,* Otto meant the conceptual, the logical, and, in a wider sense, all that is natural and ordinary in life. In his writing Otto contrasted this rational element in experience with the nonrational—the sense of the numinous we perceive by feeling and intuition.

As I have tried to show, this dichotomy is a constant in supernatural fiction. The writer of such fiction has to convince the reader that the nonrational elements in the writer's story are credible. To achieve this credibility, the author must link them carefully to a background of ordinary, or rational, events. The best of these stories exemplify what William James wrote of as the "ontological imagination": they seek to convince rather than merely to entertain.[1]

The demands of the rational have led writers of supernatural fiction to a growing reliance on realism, a development noted in the work of Edgar Allan Poe, Henry James, Bram Stoker, and more recent writers. In stories where this sense of the rational is weak, as in some of the classic Gothic novels, there is a consequent loss of power; where it is strong, however, the numinous quality of the tale is enhanced.

The demands of the rational in supernatural literature are not identical with those of ordinary realism, though, a fact sometimes misunderstood by critics. In the supernatural tale, elements of plot, character, and setting exist not for their own sake but for the sake of the nonrational dimension—the numinous. As a result some critics have misinterpreted the supernatural element, either by rationalizing it out of existence or by discussing it in purely symbolic terms. This, as I have tried to show, is to mistake the purpose of such works.

This purpose finds its clearest delineation in Otto's account of the numinous. Analysis of this *mysterium tremendum* in the works under discussion has been my chief interest in this book. Applying Otto's theory as a primary tool but using subsidiary insights from anthropology, psychology, and philosophy, I have argued that Gothic literature treats of a recognizable, albeit obscure, portion of man's existence. I have tried as well to show that this experience is particularly relevant in our own time, a period in which science and/or technology threaten to usurp man's spiritual life.

Finally, I have collected and presented evidence to refute the view that supernatural literature is morally neutral and has nothing to say about man's ethical condition. Employing Otto's concept of "the sacred and the profane," I have argued that such works as *Frankenstein, The Turn of the Screw,* and *Dracula,* while to some extent by-passing ordinary ethical problems, focus on the cosmic struggle between good and evil. Again, my purpose is to illuminate an area of Gothic literature often misunderstood in the past.

The final question I want to discuss concerns the epistemological value of the numinous experience. This is the most difficult question of all, and it takes us into a controversial area. Whereas most of Otto's commentators have conceded his success in defining the numinous experience on its subjective side, some have raised questions as to the "truth value" of the category. The question, in other words, is not whether the sense of the numinous is a *real* experience that can provide human beings with hints and probabilities about their spiritual life, but whether these hints and probabilities amount to *objective knowledge.*

The range of opinion in this matter is extreme, even among Otto's admirers. Of those who take a qualified position, Frederick R. Tennant, an eminent theologian of the past generation, is representative. In the Gifford Lectures of 1949, Tennant speaks of the numinous as "the germinal notion of the Beyond" but thinks it fails to provide clear or objective proof of religious realities.[2]

A more positive, though still skeptical, view is that of Ninian Smart, a well-known exponent of the philosophy of religious experience. Smart admits that numinous experiences occur, that people "have visions of the Other"; but the truth claims of such visions are hard to verify scientifically. Still, such experiences are important. They form a "necessary and indeed illuminating part of the human enterprise of accounting for the world in which we live."[3]

The Catholic theologian Karl Adam offers an even more positive assessment, holding that there is "an organ in our soul sensitive to the supernatural. This supernatural we grasp with our feelings in the experience of the *mysterium tremendum et fascinosum*. . . . Everyone can verify this in his own experience."[4]

These varying shades of opinion suggest that the numinous experience and its ultimate epistemological value cannot be "proved" according to the rigid demands of logic or science. Essentially, the numinous is an interpretation of the universe; its claims can be rejected without logical absurdity. Such a rejection might be costly, however. A universe in which awe, mystery, and fascination have no genuine basis for existence is scarcely the same universe we perceive at night when we gaze up at the stars.

Notes

Chapter 1

1. See, for example, Joel Porte, "In the Hands of an Angry God: Religious Terror in Gothic Fiction," *The Gothic Imagination: Essays in Dark Romanticism,* ed. G. R. Thompson (no place: Washington State University Press, 1974), pp. 42–46.

2. Otto, *The Idea of the Holy,* trans. John W. Harvey (New York: Oxford University Press), 1958.

3. Thompson, ed., *Gothic Imagination,* preface.

4. See Devendra P. Varma, *The Gothic Flame* (New York: Russell, 1957), pp. 210–13; S. L. Varnado, "The Idea of the Numinous in Gothic Literature," in Thompson, ed., *The Gothic Imagination,* pp. 11–21; Barton Levi St. Armand, *The Roots of Horror in the Fiction of H. P. Lovecraft* (Elizabethtown, N.Y.: Dragon Press, 1977), pp. 28–29.

5. Among the earliest such studies is Montague Summers's *The Gothic Quest,* a work which, like most pioneer investigations, suffers from a lack of discrimination and balance. A more helpful work is *The Haunted Castle* by the Finnish scholar Eino Railo, an analysis of the materials and origin of Gothic fiction. Other early works that still justify reading are Dorothy Scarborough's *The Supernatural in Modern English Fiction;* Edith Birkhead's

The Tale of Terror; Peter Penzoldt's *The Supernatural in Fiction;* and H. P. Lovecraft's *Supernatural Horror in Literature.*

Among recent studies of the Gothic novel, mention must be made of Devendra P. Varma's *The Gothic Flame,* a work that combines a wide knowledge of the classical Gothic period with a strong feeling for the numinous. Among other sound discussions are David Punter's thorough and enlightening *The Literature of Terror; The Gothic Imagination,* ed. G. R. Thompson; Elizabeth MacAndrew's *The Gothic Tradition in Fiction;* Coral Ann Howell's *Love, Mystery, and Misery; The Literature of the Occult,* ed. Peter B. Messent; Linda Bayer-Berenbaum's *The Gothic Imagination;* and *Horror Literature: A Core Collection and Reference Guide,* ed. Marshall B. Tymn.

Chapter 2

1. Otto, *The Idea of the Holy,* trans. John W. Harvey (New York: Oxford University Press, 1958), foreword.

2. The quotations in this and the following two paragraphs are from Otto, *Idea of the Holy,* pp. 5, 6–7, 13–16, respectively.

3. Lewis, *Problem of Pain* (New York: Macmillan, 1971), p. 17.

4. The quotations in this and the following five paragraphs are from Otto, *Idea of the Holy,* pp. 19–24, 13, 27–29, 33–34, 31, and 113–14, respectively.

5. James, *The Varieties of Religious Experience* (New York: New American Library, 1958), p. 61.

6. This quotation and those in the following eight paragraphs are from Otto, *Idea of the Holy,* pp. 67–68, 67, 67–68, 69, 51, and 51–52, respectively.

7. See Karl Adam, *The Christ of Faith: The Christology of the Church* (New York: Pantheon, 1957); Mircea Eliade, *The Sacred and the Profane* (New York: Macmillan, 1957); Carl Jung, *Psychology and Religion* (New Haven: Yale University Press, 1938); H. J. Paton, *The Modern Predicament* (London: Allen & Unwin, 1950); Ninian Smart, *The Phenomenon of Religion* (New York: Herder, 1973); Frederick R. Tennant, *Philosophical Theology*

(Cambridge: Cambridge University Press, 1956); and Joachim Wach, *Types of Religious Experience: Christian and non-Christian* (London: Routledge, 1951).

8. See Maud Bodkin, *Archetypal Patterns in Poetry: Psychological Studies of Imagination* (London: Oxford University Press, 1934); Walter Kaufman, *From Shakespeare to Existentialism: Studies in Poetry, Religion, and Philosophy* (Boston: Beacon, 1959); and Nathan A. Scott, Jr., *Modern Literature and the Religious Frontier* (New York: Harper, 1958).

Chapter 3

1. Eliade, *The Sacred and the Profane* (New York: Macmillan, 1957).
2. Ibid., pp. 203–204.
3. Quoted in Marvin Mudrick's introduction to Walpole, *The Castle of Otranto* (New York: Collier, 1963), p. 7.
4. Edith Birkhead, *The Tale of Terror* (New York: Russell, 1963), p. 19.
5. Horace Walpole, *The Castle of Otranto,* edited and with introduction by W. S. Lewis, notes by Joseph W. Reed, Jr. (Oxford: Oxford University Press, 1980), p. 7.
6. Sir Walter Scott, *Sir Walter Scott on Novelists and Fiction,* ed. Ioan Williams (New York: Barnes, 1968), p. 87.
7. Ibid., p. 87.
8. Ibid., p. 89.
9. Ibid., p. 91.
10. Varma, *The Gothic Flame* (New York: Russell, 1957), p. 66.
11. Wilt, *Ghosts of the Gothic* (Princeton: Princeton University Press, 1980), p. 25.
12. Walpole, *Castle of Otranto,* pp. 23–24.
13. Ibid., p. 102.
14. Scott, *Scott on Novelists and Fiction,* p. 92.
15. Walpole, *Castle of Otranto,* p. 108.
16. Punter, *The Literature of Terror* (London: Longman, 1980), p. 53.

17. Railo, *The Haunted Castle: A Study of the Elements of English Romanticism* (New York: Humanities Press, 1964).

18. Reeve, *Old English Baron. Seven Masterpieces of Gothic Horror,* ed. Robert D. Spector (New York: Bantam, 1963).

19. Varma, *Gothic Flame,* p. 77.

20. Reeve, *Old English Baron,* p. 106.

21. Quoted in Varma, *Gothic Flame,* p. 78.

22. Reeve, *Old English Baron,* p. 148.

23. "Walpole's sheer bravado, and his comparative freedom from moral purpose, enable him to create something which is strange even in its failures, whereas Reeve's commonsensicality, her acquiescence in a fundamentally rationalist ideology, mean that her ghosts do nothing to differentiate her book from the mainstream of eighteenth-century literature." David Punter, *Literature of Terror,* pp. 55–56.

24. Radcliffe, *Mysteries of Udolpho,* edited and with introduction by Bonamy Dobree, notes by Frederick Garber (Oxford: Oxford University Press, 1970), p. 54.

25. Burke, *A Philosophical Enquiry into the Origin of Our Ideas of the Sublime and Beautiful,* edited by T. J. Boulton (London: Routledge, 1958), pp. 57–77.

26. For a discussion of Kant, Kames, and Allison, see Samuel H. Monk, *The Sublime* (Ann Arbor: University of Michigan Press, 1960), pp. 4–9, 113–17, 148–53.

27. Otto, *The Idea of the Holy,* trans. John W. Harvey (New York: Oxford University Press, 1958), pp. 41–42.

28. Ibid., pp. 62–63.

29. Joel Porte describes the relationship between the sublime and the awesome in the novel as a "brooding sense of religious terror which is notably Protestant in its origin and bearing." "In the Hands of an Angry God: Religious Terror in Gothic Fiction," in *The Gothic Imagination: Essays in Dark Romanticism,* ed. G. R. Thompson (no place: Washington State University Press, 1974), p. 127.

30. Radcliffe, *Mysteries of Udolpho,* p. 224.

31. Ibid., pp. 226–27.

32. Eliade, *Sacred and Profane,* p. 20.

33. Ibid., pp. 36–37.

34. Ibid., pp. 40–41.

35. Otto, *Idea of the Holy,* p. 67.

36. Radcliffe, *Mysteries of Udolpho,* p. 248.

37. Varma, *Gothic Flame,* p. 95.

38. Otto, *Idea of the Holy,* p. 14.

39. Ibid., p. 122.

40. Ibid., p. 150.

41. Robert Hume, "Gothic versus Romantic," pp. 286–87, sees this quality as central to all Gothic fiction: "The key characteristic of the Gothic novel is not its devices, but its atmosphere. The atmosphere is one of evil and brooding terror."

42. Birkhead, *Tale of Terror,* p. 66.

43. Berryman, in his introduction to Matthew G. Lewis, *The Monk* (New York: Grove Press, 1952), p. 13.

44. Varma, *Gothic Flame,* p. 140.

45. Railo, *Haunted Castle,* p. 79; Summers, *The Gothic Quest* (New York: Russell, 1964), p. 222.

46. For a useful discussion of this tradition see Nicholas K. Kiessling, "Demonic Dread: The Incubus Figure in British Literature," in *Gothic Imagination,* ed. Thompson, pp. 22–41.

47. Lewis, *The Monk,* edited and with an introduction by Howard Anderson (Oxford: Oxford University Press, 1973), p. 271.

48. Ibid., p. 433.

49. Ibid., p. 434–44.

50. Of this final confrontation, Robert Kiely remarks: "In no other scene is Lewis's language so charged, his rhythm so insistent, his feelings so obviously engaged as in this last, where he smashes his own creation." *The Romantic Novel in England* (Cambridge: Harvard University Press, 1972), p. 117.

51. "Gothic machinery becomes in Maturin's hands a metaphorical language for describing new insights into human suffering and conflict," Coral Ann Howells, *Love, Mystery, and Misery: Feeling in Gothic Fiction* (London: Athlone, 1978), p. 133.

52. Charles Robert Maturin, *Melmoth the Wanderer,* introduction by William F. Axton (Lincoln: University of Nebraska Press, 1961), p. 407.

53. For a discussion of "negative romanticism," see Robert D. Hume, "Exuberant Gloom, Existential Agony, and Heroic De-

spair: Three Varieties of Negative Romanticism," in *Gothic Imagination,* pp. 109–27.

54. Dale Kramer, *Charles Robert Maturin* (New York: Twayne, 1973), p. 98.

55. Maturin, *Melmoth the Wanderer,* p. 326.

56. Edgar Allan Poe, *The Complete Works,* ed. James A. Harrison, 16 vols. (Crowell, 1902; reissued in 1965 by AMS Press), vol. 7, p. xxxviii.

57. See Robert D. Hume, "Gothic versus Romantic: A Reevaluation of the Gothic Novel," *PMLA* 84.2 (1969), p. 286.

Chapter 4

1. Sigmund Freud, *The Complete Psychological Works,* trans. and ed. James Straches, 24 vols. (London: Hogarth, 1955), vol. 17, pp. 241–43.

2. "Frankenstein is as much a philosophical novel and a vehicle of humanitarian propaganda as it is a novel of terror." Frederick S. Frank, "The Gothic Romance: 1762–1820," in *Horror Literature: A Collection and Reference Guide,* ed. Marshall B. Tymn (New York: Bowker, 1981), p. 150.

3. For a comment on the influence of Shelley, Godwin, Rousseau, and other Romantic theorists, see Robert Kiely, *The Romantic Novel in England* (Cambridge: Harvard University Press, 1972), pp. 155–57.

4. Mary Shelley, *Frankenstein or the Modern Prometheus,* ed. M. K. Joseph (Oxford: Oxford University Press, 1969), p. 162.

5. "Frankenstein's tragedy stems not from his Promethean excess, but from his own moral failure to love. He *abhorred his creature,* became terrified of it, and fled his responsibilities." Harold Bloom, "Frankenstein or the New Prometheus," *Partisan Review,* Fall 1982, pp. 613–14.

6. A good discussion of the artistry and power of the book is found in Lowry Nelson, Jr., "Night Thoughts on the Gothic Novel," *Yale Review* 52 (1962), pp. 236–57.

7. Rudolf Otto, *The Idea of the Holy,* trans. John W. Harvey (New York: Oxford University Press, 1958), p. 50.

8. Ibid., p. 51.

9. Rudolf Otto, *Religious Essays,* trans. Brian Lunn (Oxford: Oxford University Press, 1931), p. 3.

10. Marett, *The Threshold of Religion* (New York: Methuen, 1914), p. 99.

11. Eliade, *The Sacred and the Profane* (New York: Macmillan, 1957), p. 178.

12. Ibid., p. 204.

13. Shelley, *Frankenstein,* p. 37.

14. Shelley, *Frankenstein,* p. 40.

15. C. S. Lewis, *The Abolition of Man* (New York: Macmillan, 1967), pp. 87–89.

16. Shelley, *Frankenstein,* pp. 47–48.

17. Christopher Small makes some interesting suggestions as to where Mary Shelley may have encountered this version of the legend. See his *Mary Shelley's Frankenstein: Tracing the Myth* (Pittsburgh: University of Pittsburgh Press, 1973), pp. 48–59.

18. Samuel Holmes Vasbinder has collected information concerning Mary Shelley's scientific knowledge. See his *Scientific Attitudes in Mary Shelley's Frankenstein* (Ann Arbor: UMI Research Press, 1984). In *Billion Year Spree* (New York: Doubleday, 1973), pp. 7–39, Brian W. Aldiss attempts to make a case for Mary Shelley as "the first writer of science fiction."

19. Shelley, *Frankenstein;* this and the following three quotations are to pp. 51–59.

20. Small, *Mary Shelley's Frankenstein,* p. 66.

21. L. J. Swingle argues that Frankenstein is a victim of "the essential unknowableness of things; he discovers the human mind's inability to deduce truth about the essential nature of things from phenomenal data." See his "Frankenstein's Monster and Its Romantic Relatives: Problems of Knowledge in English Romanticism," *Texas Studies in Literature and Language* 15.1 (Spring 1973), pp. 51–65.

22. Shelley, *Frankenstein,* p. 55.

23. P. D. Flack attributes Frankenstein's guilt to selfishness. "It was the immoderate way in which Frankenstein sought to give shape to his dream that caused his destruction and the destruction of the dream." See "Mary Shelley's Notes to Shelley's Poems and *Frankenstein,*" *Studies in Romanticism* 6 (1967), pp. 226–54.

24. Eliade, *Sacred and Profane,* pp. 14–15.

25. Shelley, *Frankenstein;* this and the following three quotations are to pp. 97–100.

26. Quoted in Small, *Mary Shelley's Frankenstein,* p. 63.

27. Shelley, *Frankenstein;* this and the following quotations are to pp. 145–203.

28. Ibid., pp. 203, 207. For an interesting interpretation of the mountain scenery of the novel, see Linda Bayer-Berenbaum, *The Gothic Imagination: Expansion in Gothic Literature and Art* (Rutherford, N.J.: Fairleigh Dickinson University Press, 1982), pp. 139–42.

Chapter 5

1. Rudolf Otto, *Idea of the Holy,* trans. Harvey (New York: Oxford University Press, 1958), appendix, pp. 216–20.

2. Winters, *In Defense of Reason* (New York: Swallow Press, 1947), pp. 234–61.

3. Eliot, "From Poe to Valery," *Hudson Review,* August 1949, p. 335.

4. The admiration the French feel for Poe is discussed in Patrick F. Quinn's *The French Face of Edgar Poe* (Carbondale: Southern Illinois University Press, 1957).

5. Charles Pierre Baudelaire, *Baudelaire on Poe,* ed. and trans. Lois and Francis E. Hyslop, Jr. (State College, Pa.: Bald Eagle Press, 1952), p. 151.

6. This neglected side of Poe's work is discussed by Stuart Levine in his *Edgar Poe: Seer and Craftsman* (Deland, Fla.: Everett/Edwards, 1972), pp. 154–62.

7. Poe, *The Complete Works of Edgar Allan Poe,* ed. James A. Harrison, 16 vols. (Crowell, 1902; reissued in 1965 by AMS Press), vol. 16, pp. 88–91.

8. Otto, *Idea of the Holy,* p. 39.

9. Quoted in R. C. Zaehner, *Mysticism: Sacred and Profane* (New York: Oxford University Press, 1961), pp. 46–47.

10. Poe, *Complete Works,* vol. 11, pp. 71–72.

11. Ibid., vol. 14, pp. 273–74.

12. See Donald A. Ringe, *American Gothic: Imagination and*

Reason in Nineteenth-Century Fiction (Lexington: University Press of Kentucky, 1984), pp. 128–51; and David R. Saliba, *A Psychology of Fear: The Nightmare Formula of Edgar Allan Poe* (Lanham, Md.: University of America Press, 1980).

13. The neglected tale is given an original reading by David Halliburton, *Edgar Allan Poe: A Phenomenological Study* (Princeton: Princeton University Press, 1973), pp. 245–56.

14. Poe, *Complete Works,* vol. 2, pp. 1–2.

15. Ibid., p. 5.

16. Ibid., p. 6.

17. Ibid., p. 8.

18. Ibid., p. 13.

19. Ibid., pp. 13–14.

20. Jules Zanger, "Poe and the Theme of Forbidden Knowledge," *American Literature* 49.4, January 1978, pp. 533–43, connects this and several other tales by Poe with the theme of repressed sex, but his argument appears unconvincing.

21. Tate, "The Angelic Imagination," in *The Man of Letters in the Modern World* (New York: Meridian, 1955), pp. 118–19.

22. Poe, *Complete Works,* vol. 4, pp. 203–204.

23. Tate, "Angelic Imagination," p. 124.

24. Mystical and visionary elements in another of Poe's "angelic" tales, "The Conversation of Eiros and Charmion," are emphasized by Douglas Robinson, "Poe's Mini-Apocalypse: 'The Conversation of Eiros and Charmion,' " *Studies in Short Fiction,* Fall 1982, pp. 329–37.

25. G. R. Thompson's theory that Poe's work is an "ambivalent parody of the world of the Gothic horror tale" is ingenious and in some instances convincing. Thompson concedes, however, that such elements are "rarely so obtrusive as to destroy the uncanny supernatural effect." *Poe's Fiction: Romantic Irony in the Gothic Tales* (Madison: University of Wisconsin Press, 1973), pp. 65–77.

26. Poe, *Complete Works,* vol. 2, p. 225.

27. Eliade, *Sacred and Profane,* p. 38.

28. Poe, *Complete Works,* vol. 2, p. 229.

29. Ibid., pp. 237–38.

30. Ibid., p. 240.

31. Ibid.

32. Kenneth Egan sees a pattern in which descent culminates in "ascent into enlightenment." See his "Descent as Ascent: Poe's Use of Perspective in 'A Descent into the Maelstrom,' " *Studies in Short Fiction,* Spring 1982, pp. 157–62.

33. Poe, *Complete Works,* vol. 2, pp. 242–43.

34. Eliade, *Sacred and Profane,* pp. 181–82.

35. Poe, *Complete Works,* vol. 2, p. 247.

Chapter 6

1. F. W. Dupee, *Henry James* (no place: William Sloan, 1951), pp. 9–11.

2. Martha Banta, *Henry James and the Occult* (Bloomington: Indiana University Press, 1972), pp. 20–25.

3. Edel, ed., *The Ghostly Tales of Henry James* (Philadelphia: Lippincott, 1962), intro., p. v.

4. Henry James, *The Complete Tales of Henry James,* 12 vols., ed. with intro. Leon Edel (Philadelphia: Lippincott, 1962–64), vol. 4., p. 49.

5. Ibid., p. 52.

6. Ibid., p. 75.

7. Ibid., p. 77.

8. See Banta, *Henry James and the Occult,* pp. 109–10.

9. James, *The New York Edition of Henry James,* 26 vols. (New York: Scribner's, 1908; reissued in 1971 by Augustus M. Kelley), vol. 12, p. xv.

10. Ibid., p. xviii.

11. Ibid., pp. xviii–xix.

12. Ibid., p. xix.

13. Ibid.

14. Ibid., p. xx.

15. Ibid., pp. xv–xvi.

16. James, *The Notebooks of Henry James,* ed. F. O. Matthiesen and Kenneth B. Murdock (New York: Oxford University Press, 1961), pp. 178–79.

17. Quoted in Edel, ed., *Ghostly Tales of Henry James,* p. 222.

18. James, *The Letters of Henry James,* 2 vols., ed. Percy Lubbock (New York: Octagon, 1970), vol. 1, p. 299.

19. This "triple mediation" is explained by Elizabeth Mac-Andrew, *The Gothic Tradition in Fiction* (New York: Columbia University Press, 1979), p. 231; James, *New York Edition,* vol. 12, pp. 147–57.

20. "What might elsewhere be Gothic trimming is here disciplined by the pattern," Robert Heilman remarks in his " 'The Turn of the Screw' as Poem," in *A Casebook on James's "The Turn of the Screw,"* ed. Gerald Willen (New York: Crowell, 1960), p. 179.

21. James, *New York Edition,* vol. 12, pp. 162–63.

22. Woolf, *Granite and Rainbow* (New York: Harcourt, 1958), p. 71.

23. James, *New York Edition,* vol. 12, pp. 163–64.

24. Ibid., pp. 176–77.

25. Ibid., p. xxi.

26. "Good and bad are equally dubious in 'The Turn of the Screw,' though the former is emphasized and the latter hinted at." Charles Thomas Samuels, *The Ambiguity of Henry James* (Urbana: University of Illinois Press, 1971), p. 22.

27. Otto, *Religious Essays,* trans. Brian Lunn (Oxford: Oxford University Press, 1931), p. 23.

28. James, *New York Edition,* vol. 12, pp. 226–27.

29. Ibid., p. 257.

30. Ibid., pp. 259–60.

31. Wilson, "The Ambiguity of Henry James," *Hound & Horn,* April–May 1934, p. 385.

32. A good summary of this controversy is Alexander E. Jones's "Point of View in *The Turn of the Screw,*" *PMLA* 74.1 (1959), pp. 221–22. Among those who hold that ghosts are hallucinations of the governess, Jones lists Harold C. Goddard, Edna Kenton, Edmund Wilson, and Oscar Cargill; critics who dismiss the hallucination theory as untenable are Joseph Warren Beach, Carl Van Doren, F. O. Matthiesen, Kenneth Murdock, Robert Heilman, Oliver Evans, and Allen Tate.

Chapter 7

1. See Elizabeth MacAndrew, *The Gothic Tradition in Fiction* (New York: Columbia University Press, 1979); Judith Wilt, *Ghosts of the Gothic* (Princeton: Princeton University Press, 1980); Glen St. John Barclay, *Anatomy of Horror: The Masters of Occult Fiction* (New York: St. Martin's Press, 1978); David Punter, *The Literature of Terror* (London: Longman, 1980); and Leonard Wolf, ed., *The Annotated Dracula* (New York: Clarkson N. Potter, 1975).

2. Royce MacGillivray lists the strengths of the book as vividness, concision, pictorial quality of the background, and poetic language. See his " 'Dracula': Bram Stoker's Spoiled Masterpiece," *Queen's Quarterly,* Winter 1972, pp. 518–27.

3. Barclay, *Anatomy of Horror;* this and the next two quotations are found on pp. 44, 45, and 49, respectively.

4. Punter, *Literature of Terror,* pp. 256, 261.

5. Wolf, *Annotated Dracula,* p. 255.

6. Throughout, I use the Modern Library edition of *Dracula,* which carries the copyright date 1897 but no publication date of its own.

7. Stoker, *Dracula,* p. 2.

8. Ibid., p. 6.

9. The quotations in this paragraph are from ibid., pp. 9, 12.

10. Rudolf Otto, *The Idea of the Holy,* trans. John W. Harvey (New York: Oxford University Press, 1968), pp. 106–107.

11. Stoker, *Dracula,* p. 26.

12. The quotations in this paragraph are from ibid., pp. 22, 23.

13. Ibid., p. 32. Richard Wasson points out instances of this racial motif, as well as the contrast between East and West, in "The Politics of Dracula," *English Literature in Transition: 1880–1920* 9.1 (1966), pp. 24–25.

14. Raymond T. McNally and Radu Florescu, *In Search of Dracula* (New York: Warner, 1972), p. 42.

15. Quoted in Otto, *Idea of the Holy,* pp. 150–51.

16. Ibid., p. 152.

17. Royce MacGillivray, who is generally critical of Stoker's

characterizations, admits that Renfield is an exception. " 'Dracula,' " p. 525.

18. Stoker, *Dracula,* p. 111.

19. Jung, *Psychology and Religion* (New Haven: Yale University Press, 1938), p. 4.

20. Jung, "Personal and Collective Unconscious," in *Two Essays on Analytical Psychology* (Cleveland: World Publishing, 1956), p. 80.

21. Ibid., pp. 106–107.

22. Barclay, *Anatomy of Horror,* p. 45.

23. Stoker, *Dracula,* p. 20.

24. Ibid., pp. 19–20.

25. Ibid., pp. 199–200.

26. Mark M. Kennelly, Jr., sees the struggle as between "rival epistemologies in quest of a gnosis which will rehabilitate the Victorian Wasteland." *"Dracula:* The Gnostic Quest and the Victorian Wasteland," *English Literature in Transition: 1880–1920* 20.1 (1977), pp. 13–25.

27. Stoker, *Dracula,* p. 211.

28. Ibid., pp. 262–63.

29. Carol L. Fry, in an otherwise perceptive article, suggests as the reason for the novel's success the "repressed sexuality" seen in the relationship of Dracula, Mina, and Lucy. "Fictional Conventions and Sexuality in *Dracula,*" *Victorian Newsletter,* Fall 1972, pp. 20–22.

30. This pattern is noted, but is given a different interpretation, by Mark Kennelly in his "Dracula: The Gnostic Quest," p. 17.

31. Stoker, *Dracula,* pp. 264–65.

32. Judith Wilt comments: "The 'haunted castle' is the [entire] planet, and the beat of special and dangerous mysteries in one continent calls forth its answer from another." *Ghosts of the Gothic,* pp. 93–94.

33. Stoker, *Dracula,* p. 411.

34. Ibid., p. 416.

Chapter 8

1. D. P. M. Michael, *Arthur Machen* (no place: University of

Wales Press, 1971), pp. 1–12.

2. Peter Penzoldt suggests that Machen's Little People symbolize repressed sexual desire and guilt. See *The Supernatural in Fiction* (New York: Humanities Press, 1965), pp. 157–58.

3. Jack Sullivan, "Psychological, Antiquarian and Cosmic Horror: 1872–1917," *Horror Literature: A Core Collection and Reference Guide,* ed. Marshall B. Tymn (New York: R. R. Bowker, 1981), p. 237.

4. Sullivan, "Psychological, Antiquarian and Cosmic Horror," p. 255.

5. Otto, *The Idea of the Holy,* trans. John W. Harvey (New York: Oxford University Press, 1958), pp. 14–15.

6. Arthur Machen, "The Great God Pan," *The House of Souls* (Freeport, N. Y.: Books For Libraries Press, 1971), p. 170.

7. Ibid., p. 213.

8. Ibid., p. 237.

9. Otto, *Idea of the Holy,* p. 123.

10. See H. P. Lovecraft, *Supernatural Horror in Literature,* introduction by E. F. Bleiler (New York: Dover, 1973), p. 33; and Dorothy Scarborough, *The Supernatural in Modern English Fiction* (New York: Octagon, 1965), p. 247.

11. David Punter describes Blackwood's stories as evincing a "dialectic of barbarism and the civilized." *The Literature of Terror* (London: Longman, 1980), p. 331.

12. Otto, *Idea of the Holy,* pp. 235–36.

13. Ibid., pp. 126–27.

14. Algernon Blackwood, "The Willows" (originally published in *The Listener,* 1907; reissued New York: Books For Libraries, 1971), pp. 137–38.

15. Rose, *Ancient Roman Religion* (London: Hutchinson's University Library, 1948), pp. 13–15.

16. Blackwood, "The Willows," p. 147.

17. Ibid., p. 203.

18. The best account of Lovecraft's life is L. Sprague de Camp's *Lovecraft: A Biography.* Stimulating but impressionistic sketches are those of Colin Wilson and Frank Belknap Long.

19. See S. T. Joshi, ed., *H. P. Lovecraft: Four Decades of Criticism* (Athens: Ohio University Press, 1980); and Barton Levi

St. Armand, *The Roots of Horror in the Fiction of H. P. Lovecraft* (Elizabethtown, N. Y.: Dragon Press, 1977).

20. For widely differing assessments of Lovecraft's work, see Edmund Wilson, "Tales of the Marvellous and the Ridiculous," in *H. P. Lovecraft: Four Decades of Criticism,* ed. S. T. Joshi (Athens: Ohio University Press, 1980), pp. 46–49; and T. O. Mabbott, "H. P. Lovecraft: An Appreciation," in Joshi, ed., *H. P. Lovecraft,* pp. 43–45.

21. de Camp, *Lovecraft,* p. 271.

22. Lovecraft, *The Dunwich Horror and Others,* selected and with introduction by August Derleth (Sauk City, Wis.: Arkham, 1963), p. 60.

23. Ibid., p. xvi.

24. Punter, *Literature of Terror,* pp. 281–82.

25. Ibid.

26. Lovecraft, *At the Mountains of Madness and Other Novels,* selected and with an introduction by August Derleth (Sauk City, Wis.: Arkham, 1964), p. 92; and Lovecraft, *Dunwich Horror,* p. 156.

27. This idea was suggested by Peter Penzoldt, *Supernatural in Fiction,* pp. 168–69.

28. Jung, *Two Essays on Analytical Psychology* (Cleveland: World Publishing, 1956), p. 80.

29. Ibid., p. 82.

Chapter 9

1. James, *The Varieties of Religious Experience* (New York: New American Library, 1958), p. 71.

2. Tennant, *Philosophical Theology* (Cambridge: Cambridge University Press, 1956), pp. 308–11.

3. Smart, *The Phenomenon of Religion* (New York: Herder, 1973), pp. 141–48.

4. Adam, *The Christ of Faith: The Christology of the Church* (New York: Pantheon, 1957), pp. 115–19.

Bibliography

Adam, Karl. *The Christ of Faith: The Christology of the Church.* New York: Pantheon, 1957.

Aldiss, Brian W. *Billion Year Spree.* New York: Doubleday, 1973.

Banta, Martha. *Henry James and the Occult.* Bloomington: Indiana University Press, 1972.

Barclay, Glen St. John. *Anatomy of Horror: The Masters of Occult Fiction.* New York: St. Martin's Press, 1978.

Baudelaire, Charles Pierre. *Baudelaire on Poe.* Edited and translated by Lois Hyslop and Francis E. Hyslop, Jr. State College, Pa.: Bald Eagle Press, 1952.

Bayer-Berenbaum, Linda. *The Gothic Imagination: Expansion in Gothic Literature and Art.* Rutherford, N.J.: Fairleigh Dickinson University Press, 1982.

Birkhead, Edith. *The Tale of Terror.* New York: Russell, 1963.

Blackwood, Algernon. "The Willows." Originally published in *The Listener,* 1907. Reissued New York: Books For Libraries Press, 1971.

Bland, D. S. "Endangering the Reader's Neck: Background Description in the Novel." *Criticism* 2 (1961), pp. 121–39.

Bloom, Harold. "Frankenstein or the New Prometheus." *Partisan Review,* Fall 1982, pp. 611–18.

Bodkin, Maud. *Archetypal Patterns in Poetry: Psychological Studies of Imagination.* London: Oxford University Press, 1934.

Burke, Edmund. *A Philosophical Enquiry into the Origin of Our Ideas of the Sublime and Beautiful.* Edited by T. J. Boulton. London: Routledge, 1958.

de Camp, L. Sprague. *Lovecraft: A Biography.* Garden City, N.Y.: Doubleday, 1975.

Derleth, August. Introduction. *The Dunwich Horror and Others,* by H. P. Lovecraft. Sauk City, Wis.: Arkham House, 1963.

Dupee, F. W. *Henry James.* No place: William Sloan, 1951.

Edel, Leon, ed. and intro. *The Ghostly Tales of Henry James.* Philadelphia: Lippincott, 1962.

Egan, Kenneth V., Jr. "Descent as Ascent: Poe's Use of Perspective in 'A Descent into the Maelstrom.' " *Studies in Short Fiction,* Spring 1982, pp. 157–62.

Eliade, Mircea. *The Sacred and the Profane.* New York: Macmillan, 1957.

Eliot, T. S. "From Poe to Valery." *Hudson Review,* August 1949, pp. 327–43.

Flack, P. D. "Mary Shelley's Notes to Shelley's Poems and *Frankenstein.*" *Studies in Romanticism* 6 (1967), pp. 226–54.

Frank, Frederick S. "The Gothic Romance: 1762–1820." In Tymn, ed., *Horror Literature,* pp. 3–175.

Freud, Sigmund. *The Complete Psychological Works.* Translated and edited by James Strachey. 24 vols. London: Hogarth, 1955, vol. 17.

Fry, Carol L. "Fictional Conventions and Sexuality in *Dracula. Victorian Newsletter,* Fall 1972, pp. 20–22.

Halliburton, David. *Edgar Allan Poe: A Phenomenological Study.* Princeton, N.J.: Princeton University Press, 1973.

Heilman, Robert. " 'The Turn of the Screw' as Poem." *A Casebook on James's "The Turn of the Screw."* Edited by Gerald Willen. New York: Crowell, 1960.

Howells, Coral Ann. *Love, Mystery, and Misery: Feeling in Gothic Fiction.* London: Athlone, 1978.

Hume, Robert D. "Exuberant Gloom, Existential Agony, and Heroic Despair: Three Varieties of Negative Romanticism." In Thompson, ed., *Gothic Imagination,* pp. 109–27.

———. "Gothic Versus Romantic: A Reevaluation of the Gothic Novel." *PMLA* 84.2 (1969), pp. 282–90.

James, Henry. *The Complete Tales of Henry James.* Edited with an introduction by Leon Edel. 12 vols. Philadelphia: Lippincott, 1962–64, vol. 4.

———. *The Letters of Henry James.* Edited by Percy Lubbock. 2 vols. New York: Octagon, 1970, vol. 1.

———. *The New York Edition of Henry James.* 26 vols. New York: Scribner's, 1908, vol. 12.

———. *The Notebooks of Henry James.* Edited by F. O. Matthiesen and Kenneth B. Murdock. New York: Oxford University Press, 1961.

James, M. R. "Oh, Whistle and I'll Come to You, My Lad." *Great Tales of Terror and the Supernatural.* Edited by Herbert A. Wise and Phyllis Fraser. New York: Modern Library, 1944, pp. 539–59.

James, William. *The Varieties of Religious Experience.* New York: New American, 1958.

Jones, Alexander E. "Point of View in *The Turn of the Screw.*" *PMLA* 74.1 (1959), pp. 112–22.

Joshi, S. T., ed. *H. P. Lovecraft: Four Decades of Criticism.* Athens, Ohio: Ohio University Press, 1980.

Jung, Carl. *Psychology and Religion.* New Haven: Yale University Press, 1938.

———. *Two Essays on Analytical Psychology.* Cleveland, Ohio: World Publishing, 1956.

Kaufman, Walter. *From Shakespeare to Existentialism: Studies in Poetry, Religion and Philosophy.* Boston: Beacon, 1959.

Kennelly, Mark M. "*Dracula:* The Gnostic Quest and the Victorian Wasteland." *English Literature in Transition: 1880–1920* 20.1 (1977), pp. 13–25.

Kiely, Robert. *The Romantic Novel in England.* Cambridge: Harvard University Press, 1972.

Kiessling, Nicolas K. "Demonic Dread: The Incubus Figure in British Literature." In Thompson, ed., *Gothic Imagination,* pp. 22–41.

Kramer, Dale. *Charles Robert Maturin.* New York: Twayne, 1973.

Levine, Stuart. *Edgar Poe: Seer and Craftsman.* Deland, Fla.: Everett/Edwards, 1972.

Lewis, C. S. *The Abolition of Man*. New York: Macmillan, 1967.
———. *The Problem of Pain*. New York: Macmillan, 1971.
Lewis, Matthew Gregory. *The Monk*. Introduction by John Berryman. New York: Grove Press, 1952.
———. *The Monk*. Edited and with an introduction by Howard Anderson. Oxford: Oxford University Press, 1973.
Long, Frank Belknap. *Howard Phillip Lovecraft: Dreamer on the Night Side*. Sauk City, Wis.: Arkham, 1975.
Lovecraft, H. P. *At the Mountains of Madness and Other Novels*. Selected and with an introduction by August Derleth. Sauk City, Wis.: Arkham, 1964.
———. *The Dunwich Horror and Others*. Selected by and with an introduction by August Derleth. Sauk City, Wis.: Arkham, 1963.
———. *Supernatural Horror in Literature*. Introduction by E. F. Bleiler. New York: Dover, 1973.
Mabbott, T. O. "H. P. Lovecraft: An Appreciation." In Joshi, ed., *H. P. Lovecraft*, pp. 43–45.
MacAndrew, Elizabeth. *The Gothic Tradition in Fiction*. New York: Columbia University Press, 1979.
MacGillivray, Royce. " 'Dracula': Bram Stoker's Spoiled Masterpiece." *Queen's Quarterly*, Winter 1972, pp. 518–27.
Machen, Arthur. *The House of Souls*. Originally published 1922; Freeport, N.Y.: Books For Libraries Press, 1971.
McNally, Raymond T., and Radu Florescu. *In Search of Dracula*. New York: Warner, 1972.
Marett, Robert Ranulph. *The Threshold of Religion*. New York: Methuen, 1914.
Maturin, Charles Robert. *Melmoth the Wanderer*. Introduction by William F. Axton. Lincoln: University of Nebraska Press, 1961.
Messent, Peter B., ed. *Literature of the Occult*. Englewood Cliffs, N.J.: Prentice-Hall, 1981.
Michael, D. P. M. *Arthur Machem*. No place: University of Wales Press, 1971.
Monk, Samuel H. *The Sublime*. Ann Arbor: University of Michigan Press, 1960.
Nelson, Lowry, Jr. "Night Thoughts on the Gothic Novel." *Yale Review* 52 (1962), pp. 236–57.

Otto, Rudolf. *The Idea of the Holy.* Translated by John W. Harvey. New York: Oxford University Press, 1958.

———. *Religious Essays.* Translated by Brian Lunn. Oxford: Oxford University Press, 1931.

Paton, H. J. *The Modern Predicament.* London: Allen & Unwin, 1950.

Penzoldt, Peter. *The Supernatural in Fiction.* New York: Humanities Press, 1965.

Poe, Edgar Allan. *The Complete Works of Edgar Allan Poe.* Edited by James A. Harrison. 16 vols. Crowell, 1902; reissued by AMS Press, 1965, vols. 2, 4, 11, 14, 16.

Porte, Joel. "In the Hands of an Angry God: Religious Terror in Gothic Fiction." In Thompson, ed., *Gothic Imagination,* pp. 42–64.

Punter, David. *The Literature of Terror.* London: Longman, 1980.

Quinn, Patrick F. *The French Face of Edgar Poe.* Carbondale: Southern Illinois University Press, 1957.

Radcliffe, Ann. *The Mysteries of Udolpho.* Edited by and with an introduction by Bonamy Dobree; notes by Frederick Garber. Oxford: Oxford University Press, 1970.

Railo, Eino. *The Haunted Castle: A Study of the Elements of English Romanticism.* New York: Humanities Press, 1964.

Reeve, Clara. *The Old English Baron. Seven Masterpieces of Gothic Horror.* Edited by Donald Spector. New York: Bantam, 1963, pp. 103–236.

Ringe, Donald. *American Gothic: Imagination and Reason in Nineteenth-Century Fiction.* Lexington: University Press of Kentucky, 1984.

Robinson, Douglas. "Poe's Mini-Apocalypse: The Conversation of Eiros and Charmion." *Studies in Short Fiction,* Fall 1982, pp. 329–37.

Rose, Herbert Jennings. *Ancient Roman Religion.* London: Hutchinson's University Library, 1948.

Saliba, David R. *A Psychology of Fear: The Nightmare Formula of Edgar Allan Poe.* Lanham, Md.: University Press of America, 1980.

Samuels, Charles Thomas. *The Ambiguity of Henry James.* Urbana: University of Illinois Press, 1971.

Scarborough, Dorothy. *The Supernatural in Modern English Fiction*. New York: Octagon, 1967.

Scott, Nathan A., Jr. *Modern Literature and the Religious Frontier*. New York: Harper, 1958.

Scott, Sir Walter. *Sir Walter Scott on Novelists and Fiction*. Edited by Ioan Williams. New York: Barnes, 1968.

Shelley, Mary. *Frankenstein or the Modern Prometheus*. Edited by M. K. Joseph. Oxford: Oxford University Press, 1969.

Small, Christopher. *Mary Shelley's Frankenstein: Tracing the Myth*. Pittsburgh: University of Pittsburgh Press, 1973.

St. Armand, Barton Levi. *The Roots of Horror in the Fiction of H. P. Lovecraft*. Elizabethtown, N.Y.: Dragon Press, 1977.

Stoker, Bram. *Dracula*. New York: Modern Library, n.d. Copyright 1897.

Sullivan, Jack. "Psychological, Antiquarian and Cosmic Horror: 1872–1917." In Tymn, ed., *Horror Literature*, pp. 221–75.

Summers, Montague. *The Gothic Quest*. New York: Russell, 1964.

Swingle, L. J. "Frankenstein's Monster and Its Romantic Relatives: Problems of Knowledge in English Romanticism." *Texas Studies in Literature and Language* 15.1 (Spring 1973), pp. 51–65.

Tate, Allen. "The Angelic Imagination." In *The Man of Letters in the Modern World*. New York: Meridian, 1955, pp. 113–31.

Tennant, Frederick R. *Philosophical Theology*. Cambridge: Cambridge University Press, 1956.

Thompson, G. R. *Poe's Fiction: Romantic Irony in the Gothic Tales*. Madison: University of Wisconsin Press, 1973.

———, ed. *The Gothic Imagination: Essays in Dark Romanticism*. No place: Washington State University Press, 1974.

Tymn, Marshall B., ed. *Horror Literature: A Core Collection and Reference Guide*. New York: Bowker, 1981.

Varma, Devendra P. *The Gothic Flame*. New York: Russell, 1957.

Varnado, S. L. "The Idea of the Numinous in Gothic Literature." In Thompson, ed., *Gothic Imagination*, pp. 11–21.

Vasbinder, Samuel Holmes. *Scientific Attitudes in Mary Shelley's Frankenstein*. Ann Arbor, Mich.: UMI Research Press, 1984.

Wach, Joachim. *Types of Religious Experience: Christian and non-Christian.* London: Routledge, 1951.

Walpole, Horace. *The Castle of Otranto.* Introduction by Marvin Mudrick. New York: Collier, 1963.

———. *The Castle of Otranto.* Edited and with an introduction by W. S. Lewis; notes by Joseph W. Reed, Jr. Oxford, Oxford University Press, 1980.

Wasson, Richard. "The Politics of Dracula." *English Literature in Transition: 1880–1920* 9.1 (1966), pp. 24–27.

Willen, Gerald, ed. *A Casebook on Henry James's "The Turn of the Screw."* New York: Crowell, 1960.

Wilson, Colin. *The Strength to Dream: Literature and Imagination.* Boston: Houghton Mifflin, 1962.

Wilson, Edmund. "The Ambiguity of Henry James." *Hound & Horn,* April–May 1934, pp. 385–406.

———. "Tales of the Marvellous and the Ridiculous." In Joshi, ed., *H. P. Lovecraft,* pp. 46–49.

Wilt, Judith. *Ghosts of the Gothic.* Princeton, N.J.: Princeton University Press, 1980.

Winters, Yvor. *In Defense of Reason.* New York: Swallow Press, 1947.

Wolf, Leonard, ed. *The Annotated Dracula.* By Bram Stoker. New York: Clarkson N. Potter, 1975.

Woolf, Virginia. *Granite and Rainbow.* New York: Harcourt, 1958.

Zaehner, R. C. *Mysticism: Sacred and Profane.* New York: Oxford University Press, 1961.

Zanger, Jules. "Poe and the Theme of Forbidden Knowledge." *American Literature* 49.4, January 1978, pp. 533–43.

Index

Adam, Karl, 133
Agrippa, Cornelius, 48
Albertus Magnus, 58
Alienum, 12
Alison, Archibald, 30
Anselm, Saint, 8
Archetypes: and the numinous, 108;
    Carl Jung on, 127–28
Augustine, Saint, 9

Baudelaire, Charles, 61
Blackwood, Algernon: settings of
    tales, 120; sense of "presence" in
    tales, 120; "The Willows," analy-
    sis of, 121–23
Blatty, William P., 129
Burke, Edmund, 29–30

"Call of Cthulhu, The," 127. *See
    also* Lovecraft, H. P.
Campbell, Ramsey, 129
Castle of Otranto, The: origin of, 21;
    analysis of, 23–26; assessment of,
    26
Ceremonies, The, 129. *See also* Klein,
    T. E. D.
Channing, William Ellery, 80

Coleridge, Samuel Taylor: "willing
    suspension of disbelief," 5–6, 83
"Colloquy of Monos and Una":
    analysis of, 69–70. *See also* Poe,
    Edgar Allan

Daemonic, the: in *The Monk,* 34–
    36; Goethe on, 103–104
Demon, the: Jungian archetype of,
    in *Dracula,* 108
"Descent into the Maelstrom, A":
    analysis of, 71–76. *See also* Poe,
    Edgar Allan
Dracula: Christian symbolism in,
    97–98; alleged weaknesses of,
    97–98; ideograms in, 98; analysis
    of, 98–114; racial theme in, 102–
    103; rational and nonrational in,
    110; cosmic theme in, 110–11.
    See also Stoker, Bram

Edel, Leon: on Henry James's
    ghostly tales, 79
Eliade, Mircea: "nonreligious man,"
    20–21, 26; sacred space, 32–
    33; sacred and profane, 54; "de-

sacralizing tendencies" in modern society, 69; rites of passage, 75

Eliot, T. S.: on Edgar Allan Poe, 61

Emerson, Ralph Waldo, 9; on Edgar Allan Poe, 61

Energy: as element in numinous, 12

Exorcist, The, 129. *See also* Blatty, William P.

Faerie Queene, The, 5

Fantasy: definition of, 4; contrasted with supernatural literature, 4; nature of, 5

Fascinans: as element in the numinous, 13–14; in poetry of Edgar Allan Poe, 64; in Poe's "A Descent into the Maelstrom," 74–75

Fichte, Johann Gottlieb, 12

Frankenstein: romantic elements in, 44–45; analysis of, 47–59; supposed moral ambiguity of, 44–45, 48, 53–54; sacred and profane symbolism in, 53, 58–59; scenery in, 59, *See also* Shelley, Mary

Freud, Sigmund: use of his terminology, 8; on "the uncanny," 44; sexual sublimation, 128

"Ghostly Rental, The": analysis of, 79–83. *See also* James, Henry

Godwin, William, 44

Goethe, Johann Wolfgang von, 12

Golden Fleece, The, 4

Gothic novel: supposed lack of moral purpose in, 1–3, 42; religious elements in, 26; stereotypes in, 26–27

Great God Pan, The: analysis of, 117–19; use of "horror" in, 118–19

Harmony of contrasts: in numinous, 13–14; in Poe's work, 65; in

Poe's "A Descent into the Maelstrom," 74

Harvey, Leonard: numinous elements in Romantic literature, 60

Haunted castle: as theme in Gothic novel, 32–33

Hobbit, The, 4

Horror: use of in *The Great God Pan,* 118–19; as element in numinous, 118; in work of H. P. Lovecraft, 127

Idea of the Holy, The, 1, 9, 44, 60, 89, 101, 119; analysis of the numinous in, 9–19 passim; distinction between numinous and "the holy," 15; use of concepts by other writers, 19. *See also* Otto, Rudolf

Ideogram: definition of, 9

Jackson, Shirley, 128

James, Henry: realism in work, 77; numinous element in work, 77–78; "Romance of Certain Old Clothes," 79; "The Ghostly Rental," analysis of, 79–83; realism in ghostly tales, 83; on "scientific" ghost stories, 83–84; "roundness" in ghostly tales, 84–86; character of governess in *The Turn of the Screw,* 88; use of "frame story" in *The Turn of the Screw,* 88–89

James, Henry, Sr.: interest in supernatural, 78–79

James, M. R.: "Oh, Whistle and I'll Come to You My Lad," analysis of, 42–43

James, William: sense of objective presence in consciousness, 15–16; "nature mysticism," 62; interest in psychic phenomena, 79; "ontological imagination," 131

Jeffries, Richard: nature mysticism, 63–64
Johnson, Samuel, 95
Jung, Carl: on the numinous, 107, 128; relation of archetypes to numinous, 107–108; the irrational, 128

Kames, Lord, 30
Kant, Immanuel, 9, 30
King, Stephen, 129
Klein, T. E. D.: *The Ceremonies,* 129

Levin, Ira: *Rosemary's Baby,* 129–30
Lewis, C. S., 4; description of numinous, 11; birth of modern science, 49
Lewis, Matthew Gregory: *The Monk,* analysis of, 35–38; occult tradition, 36; daemonic element in *The Monk,* 36–38
Lovecraft, H. P.: as a cult figure, 123; evaluation by critics, 124; New England background of tales, 124–26; "Cthulhu mythos," 124–25; prose style, 125–26; on supernatural literature, 126; "The Call of Cthulhu," 127; *At the Mountains of Madness,* 127; relation of work to Jungian archetypes, 127–28
Luther, Martin, 9

Machen, Arthur: Welsh background of his tales, 115–16; mythological themes in his tales, 116; occult tradition, 116; *The Great God Pan,* analysis of, 117–19; use of "horror," 118–19
Magic: in relation to numinous, 15–16; use in *The Monk,* 16. See *also* Occult
Majestas: as element in numinous, 12

"Manuscript Found in a Bottle": analysis of, 66–69. See *also* Poe, Edgar Allan
Marett, R. R.: *mana* and *tabu,* 47
Marginalia, 62. See *also* Poe, Edgar Allan
Maturin, Charles Robert: *Melmoth the Wanderer,* analysis of, 38–41; critical assessment of, 40; influence on later writers, 40
Melmoth the Wanderer: daemonic element in, 38–39; analysis of, 38–41; influence on later writers, 40; comment on by Poe, 41. See *also* Maturin, Charles Robert
Milton, John, 50
Monk, The: daemonic element in, 34–36; critical assessment of, 35; position among Gothic novels, 35–36; analysis of, 35–38; occult tradition in, 36. See *also* Lewis, Matthew Gregory
More, Paul Elmer: on Poe, 61
Mountains of Madness, At the, 127. See *also* Lovecraft, H. P.
Mysteries of Udolpho, The, 28; use of Sublime in, 29–31; analysis of, 29–34. See *also* Radcliffe, Ann
Mysterium tremendum et fascinans: as ideogram for numinous, 10; analysis of, 10–14. See *also* Numinous, the

Narnia, tales of, 4
Nature mysticism, 62–63
Negative numinous: definition of, 34–35; in *The Monk,* 35; in *The Turn of the Screw,* 86; relation to idea of the Devil, 101; in *Dracula,* 101–102; in tales of Arthur Machen, 116. See *also* Daemonic, the; Profane, the; Otto, Rudolf
Newman, John Henry, 9
Nonrational, 9, 131. See *also* Otto, Rudolf

Numinous, the: as essence of supernatural literature, 1, 6, 132; analysis of, 9–18 passim; definition
of, 10, 15; harmony of contrasts
in, 13–14; objectivity of, 14–
15; relation to "the holy," 15;
relation to the preternatural, 15–
16; artistic means of producing,
16–17, 89; as a "value category,"
17–19, 45–47, 132; in *The
Monk,* 34–35; in Buddhism, 63;
in poetry of Poe, 64; as setting
in ghostly tales, 89; in *The Turn of
the Screw,* 91; element of "horror"
in, 118; sense of "haunted presence" in, 120; in Roman religion,
121–22; objective knowledge of,
132–33. *See also* Daemonic,
the; Negative numinous; Profane,
the; *Mysterium tremendum et fascinans;* Otto, Rudolf

Occult: in work of M. G. Lewis, 36–
38; in work of Arthur Machen,
166
"Oh, Whistle and I'll Come to You
My Lad," analysis of, 42–43. *See
also* James, M. R.
Old English Baron, The: analysis of,
27–28. *See also* Reeve, Clara
Ontological imagination, 131. *See
also* James, William
Order of the Golden Dawn, the, 36,
116
Otto, Rudolf: use of concepts in
analysis of supernatural literature,
1; holiness, 9; the nonrational, 9;
concept of the numinous, 9–18
passim; the fear of ghosts, 13; use
of concepts by others, 19; on
Gothic architecture, 33; the daemonic in relation to the numinous,
34–36; numinous in Buddhism,
63; concept of "lostness," 92; on
"horror," 119; sense of "haunted

presence," 120. *See also* Daemonic, the; *Mysterium tremendum
et fascinans;* Negative numinous;
Profane, the

Paracelsus, Philippus Aureolus, 48,
49
Paradise Lost: use in *Frankenstein,*
50
Pascal, Blaise, 9
Poe, Edgar Allan: comment on *Melmoth the Wanderer,* 41; lack of
maturity, 61; *Marginalia,* 62; as a
mystic, 62–64; numinous element
in work, 62–66; ideality, 64;
sensational quality of tales, 65;
pattern of tales, 65–66; "Manuscript Found in a Bottle," analysis
of, 66–68; "Colloquy of Monos
and Una," analysis of, 69–70; "A
Descent into the Maelstrom,"
analysis of, 71–76
Preternatural, the: in Gothic architecture, 33; relation to numinous,
15–16
Problem of Pain, The, 11. *See also*
Lewis, C. S.
Profane, the: relation to numinous,
18–19. *See also* Negative
numinous
Prometheus: in *Frankenstein,* legend
of, 50

Radcliffe, Ann: *The Mysteries of
Udolpho,* 28; use of Sublime, 29–
31; *The Mysteries of Udolpho,*
analysis of, 29–34
Realism: in work of Henry James,
87–88; in supernatural tale, 131
Reeve, Clara: *The Old English Baron,*
analysis of, 27–28
Romantic literature: numinous elements in, 60
Rose, Herbert Jennings: numinous
in Roman religion, 121–22

Rosemary's Baby, 129. *See also* Levin, Ira

Sacred, the: 18–19. *See also* Numinous, the
St. Armand, Barton Levy: use of Otto's theory, 6
Schleiermacher, Friedrich, 9
Scholastics, medieval, 8
Schopenhauer, Arthur, 12
Scott, Sir Walter: on *The Castle of Otranto,* 21–22
Shelley, Mary: radical philosophy of, 44; moral ambivalence of *Frankenstein,* 45; *Frankenstein,* analysis of, 47–59
Shelley, Percy Bysshe: moral view of *Frankenstein,* 56–57
"Sleeping Beauty, The," 4
Small, Christopher: ambiguity in *Frankenstein,* 53–54
Smart, Ninian, 133
Society for Psychical Research, 79, 84, 85
Spenser, Edmund, 5
Stoker, Bram: *Dracula,* popularity of, 95; daemonic in *Dracula,* 101–104; *Dracula,* analysis of, 98–114; *Dracula,* use of legendary associations in, 102–104; use of type characters, 105; prose style, 113–14
Straub, Peter, 129
Supernatural literature: classical, 3; nineteenth century, 4; contrast with fantasy, 5; moral element in, 42–44; H. P. Lovecraft on, 126; decline in early twentieth century,

115; contemporary, 128; relation to realism, 131
Swedenborg, Emanuel, 78

Tate, Allen: on Poe as a transitional figure in literature, 69; on "Colloquy of Monos and Una," 70
Tennant, Frederic R., 133
Tolkien, J. R. R., 4
Turn of the Screw, The: origin of, 86–87; analysis of, 86–94; numinous setting of, 88–89; concept of "lostness" in, 92; critical comments on, 93; reality of ghosts in, 94. *See also* James, Henry

Varma, Devendra P.: use of Otto's concept of numinous, 6; surrealism in *The Castle of Otranto,* 22; on *The Mysteries of Udolpho,* 34
Vlad Tepes, 103

Waite, A. E., 116
Walpole, Horace: his vision of the nonrational, 20; *The Castle of Otranto,* origin of, 21; *The Castle of Otranto,* analysis of, 23–26
Wells, Herbert George, 88
Wholly other, the, 12–13
"Willows, The," analysis of, 121–23. *See also* Blackwood, Algernon
Wilson, Edmund: on *The Turn of the Screw,* 93–94
Woolf, Virginia: on *The Turn of the Screw,* 89

Zaehner, R. C.: *Mysticism Sacred and Profane,* 63

About the Author

S. L. Varnado is Professor of English, University of
South Alabama. He received his bachelor's degree from Millsaps
College, his master's from Tulane University, and his doctorate
from Fordham University.

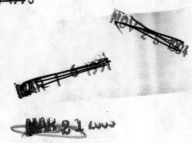